"Jim Conlon offers us a path to discovering the story of our own lives that will connect us to the emerging, cosmic Universe Story. *Earth Story, Sacred Story* is a practical book that presents meditations and questions to help us root our concerns for justice in a compassionate respect for Earth and all of its species. It works!"

Matthew Fox
Friends of Creation Spirituality

"In *Earth Story, Sacred Story* Conlon provides a way to wrestle with the deeper meaning of the New Story [about Earth]. This book will be appreciated by those who have been studying the New Story and want to reflect on its personal and social implications."

Brian Swimme
California Institute of Integral Studies

"James Conlon's new book, *Earth Story, Sacred Story*, is a powerful critique of the patterns that have created alienation between humans and the destruction of Earth. Most of all, it is a stirring vision of how to fashion a new culture, new patterns of relationships between human beings, particularly between men and women."

Rosemary Radford Ruether
Garrett-Evangelical Seminary

"In *Earth Story, Sacred Story* James Conlon deftly weaves many of the strands of the new vision that individuals and communities need as they attempt to live in greater harmony with themselves, Earth, and the divine. We are indebted to him...."

Sean McDonagh
Author, *To Care for the Earth* and *The Greening of the Church*

"*Earth Story, Sacred Story* unfolds the New Story of the universe given to us by science and probes the implications of that story for our personal lives and the way we restructure society and culture. The chapter on the interconnectedness of all things and on compassion is excellent!"

John Surette, S.J.
Director, Spiritearth, A Center for the Sacred Universe

"Jim Conlon highlights the role and importance of 'story' in arriving at a new 'sacred story' in our era. He points to possibilities for personal and cultural transformation into a new human-Earth relationship. It is important to absorb his message."

Jane Blewett
Director, Earth Community Center

"*Earth Story, Sacred Story* offers a new paradigm of being in the world. In this brilliant, timely, often challenging work, Conlon guides us to embrace the wisdom of Earth, a wisdom replete with healing and new life."

Richard Weber
Gethsemane Abbey, Kentucky

"A friend gave me a trilobite, 580 million years old. This fossil means more to me now after reading *Earth Story, Sacred Story*. After reading this book, my toothbrush also means more to me. This book makes one more alive to both nature and culture. It is a hands-on workbook for people who are serious about renewing our culture from the roots up."

David Stendl-Rast
Author, *A Listening Heart*

"*Earth Story, Sacred Story* makes clear the importance of understanding the new scientific story of creation as a communication of divine action. When culture fails to understand this, it becomes cut off from its people and the planet."

McGregor Smith
Earth Literacy Communion

"In *Earth Story, Sacred Story* the reader is invited to expand his or her horizons to a broader concern called Earth justice. The very purpose of this work is to go beyond anthropocentrism."

Edmund Sullivan
Ontario Institute for Studies in Education

"James Conlon helps individuals and groups to develop a spirituality of Earth. Central to this is what he calls geo-justice, a preferential option for Earth. He recognizes that not only must the culture be changed, but individuals as well."

Eleanor Rae, Ph.D.
Author, *Women, the Earth, the Divine*

"Conlon explores a spirituality of Earth that places our deepest human searching within a spiritual process which is the universe itself. In his celebration of the uniqueness, interiority, and communion/bonding of all beings he leads us to a new way of perceiving Earth, our culture, and ourselves."

Mary Whelan
Founding Member, Community Action Network

Foreword by Thomas Berry

EARTH STORY

SACRED STORY

JAMES CONLON

XXIII
TWENTY-THIRD PUBLICATIONS
Mystic, Connecticut 06355

The following excerpts that have been reproduced in this book are acknowledged by the author with gratitude:

Page 1: Excerpt from Pierre Teilhard de Chardin, *Hymn of the Universe*, © 1961 Harper Torchbooks, New York.

Pages 13–16: "The Creation," from *God's Trombones* by James Weldon Johnson. © 1927 The Viking Press, Inc., renewed © 1955 by Grace Nail Johnson. Used by permission of Viking Penguin, a division of Penguin Books U.S.A., Inc.

Page 90: Excerpt from Gary Snyder's "Ah to be alive," © Farrar, Straus, & Giroux, New York.

Pages 97–98: United Nations Environmental Sabbath Program.

Page 120: Adrienne Rich's "My heart is moved by all," from *The Dream of a Common Language: Poems 1974–77*, © 1978 W.W. Norton, New York.

Pages 130–131: *Earth Covenant: A Citizens' Treaty for Common Ecological Security*, © Global Education Associates, New York.

Pages 131–133: "Earth, Sister Earth," from *Sister Earth: Ecology & the Spirit* by Helder Camara, © 1990 by New City Press, New York.

Twenty-Third Publications
185 Willow Street
P.O. Box 180
Mystic, CT 06355
(203) 536-2611
800-321-0411

ISBN 0-89622-583-6
Library of Congress Catalog Card Number 93-60951
Printed in the U.S.A.

Foreword

Origins are fascinating not only because they are so mysterious but because they are so important in understanding things. We explain things by telling their story—how they came into being and the changes that have taken place over the course of time, whether minutes or millennia. But the most significant moment in any mode of being is the origin moment, the time when it was not and then came into being. Once a thing is in existence we can follow the transformations that take place as it passes through a sequence of events, either interior transformation or transformations due to exterior influences. The more important the reality, the more significant the history.

This is especially true in explaining those profound formative influences that have shaped our sense of the sacred, for this is the ultimate normative referent for our sense of reality and value. Out of this sense of the sacred we shape our life discipline, our norms of social behavior, our explanation of life, how we relate to one another and to the wider world around us.

Out of such considerations as these, this story of cultural rebirth and hope has come. One of the greatest difficulties we are experiencing in this late twentieth century is a certain dislocation in our sense of the sacred. It is little wonder that we are living such distraught lives. Our cultural formation is no longer offering adequate guidance in our sense of the sacred or in the shaping of a personal or social life discipline. The context of life has been so profoundly altered in the transition from the earlier religious and cultural context of our Western traditions that we hardly know what to think or how to act or where to find that entrancing life fulfillment that we desire deep within our being.

In resolving such basic issues the only adequate solution is to return to the source. We have tried to do this in terms of our Western religious and cultural traditions. This has not been effective because these traditions have not been able to adapt adequately to the changes in our understanding of the world about us. A profound transformation has taken place in human consciousness. We now know the world about us primarily through an empirical model of understanding. Thus when we "return to the source" we return through our observational inquiry into the origin, structure, and functioning of the universe. The traditional way of returning to the source is through scriptural or philosophical texts that tell us of creation in terms used long centuries ago with only the knowledge that existed at that time. Now, without neglecting this earlier way of returning to the source, we have a new way of understanding how things emerged in the beginning and the sequence of transformations that have led up to the present.

Each of these two models of returning to the source has its own special value. But our problems at present are such that we have a special need for the information communicated to us through this more recent way of understanding. It is the context of contemporary education. The difficulty is that this new way of understanding has neglected the depth of its own inner meaning. It has assumed that only quantitative measurements communicate the reality of things. Thus a misunderstanding has occurred, because the universe in fact presents itself as full of mystery and meaning. This has been immediately evident to the poets and artists and philosophers and mystics of all ages.

The purpose of *Earth Story, Sacred Story* is to bring about a more adequate interpretation of returning to the source in a modern understanding of this process. In this new context we understand that there is a qualitative as well as a quantitative dimension of the universe from the beginning. Even from the primordial flaring forth there was a consciousness as well as a physical dimension to the universe and to everything in it. The simplest way of explaining this is that the world of living being, of sensation and intellection, even the thinking processes of the scientists themselves, have all emerged from the primordial moment of the universe. In the process they reveal the universe to itself. We know what a thing is by what it is able to do. The universe as a whole is implicated in every manifestation and every activity of the universe. That the universe has produced sensation, imagination, thought, and feeling is sufficient evidence that the universe has immense and wonderful powers beyond any statistical measurement.

Once we understand this we can understand what returning to the source means in this story of rebirth and hope. It means especially that the basic norms of human activities can be discovered from within this profoundly spiritual process that is the universe itself. That the universe is integral with itself is what enables the universe to be a "cosmos," an "order," a comprehensive order perceived and acted upon by every child from its earliest moment of conscious life.

For the human to be integral with this universe is the first law of existence. It is an exciting thing to realize that we have an immediate presence to every being in the universe individually and to the universe itself in its unity. Every atom is immediately present to every other atom in the universe. This total identity of the universe with itself was recognized by the earliest peoples of the Paleolithic period. They experienced this identity, and it gave to them a sense of security amid the terrors of existence in a world that was as harsh in its demands as it was benign in its gifts. But above all, it was creative, and participation in this creativity was a primary experience of the human.

When we ask further what this involves as regards cultural renewal in our times, we can immediately answer that the basic laws of the universe are found in the three basic tendencies of the universe: differentiation, interiority, and communion. These are the three basic values.

First, the ultimate, unique value of the individual being. No two leaves are the same, no two snowflakes, no two grains of sand. At the human level this unique quality reaches dramatic expression.

From it flows respect for the individual, regard for personal rights. Second, there is the inner spontaneity of each being, the capacity of each being to articulate its own inner structure, to declare itself to the entire universe, and to be present to the universe in a comprehensive manner. Every being needs to listen to every other being. As humans, we need especially to listen to the manifold voices of Earth and of the entire universe. Consequent on this is the third basic law of the universe: the comprehensive bonding of each reality with every other reality. This law of intimacy of things with one another is of immense importance. It is the final expression of the curvature of space that holds all things together in a compassionate embrace that is the universe itself.

From these few comments the governing thought of *Earth Story, Sacred Story* can be appreciated. Our cultural formation is not of yesterday, nor is it derived simply from our Western or even our human traditions, nor is it simply from Earth. It is truly from time immemorial, from the farthest reaches of the universe, from the original flaring forth of the universe itself. The cultural vessels of all the peoples of Earth, however diverse, were shaped and fired in that same primordial furnace.

Thomas Berry

Contents

Acknowledgments

I thank you and I say how proud
that I have been by fate allowed
To stand here having the joyful chance
to claim my inheritance.

Patrick Kavanagh

I celebrate with gratitude my origins and ancestors: the galaxies, Earth, trees, ocean, and land; my family who came to Canada from Ireland and France

My parents, Richard and Elizabeth, who gave me life and love and roots

Thomas Berry and Matthew Fox who have connected us to the wisdom of the cosmos and the deep wells of our traditions

To all who befriend creation and practice liberation for people and Earth

The women and men of the Institute in Culture and Creation Spirituality, its students, faculty, and staff

To the Regional Connectors in Creation Spirituality and all who have been my companions and colleagues on this journey

Connie Krautkremer, John Gallagher, Debra Floyd, Lori Zook, Cathryn Farrell, Phyllis Park, and Marilyn Goddard, who have worked with me on this book

Joan Marie LaFlamme, without whose considerable contribution and assistance these pages would not have become a book

Neil Kluepfel, Gwen Costello, John van Bemmel, and the staff of Twenty-Third Publications whose support, guidance, and good work have brought this book to publication

And each of you whose story is sacred and whose purpose and destiny profound.

The day will come when after harnessing space
the wind
the tides
and gravitation
We will harness for God the energies of love

And on that day for the second time in the history
of the world
We shall have discovered fire.

Pierre Teilhard de Chardin[1]

Introduction

Blessed be you, mighty matter, irresistible march of evolution, reality ever new-born; you who, by constantly shattering our mental categories, force us to go ever further and further in our pursuit of the truth.

Pierre Teilhard de Chardin[1]

By all accounts, we are living in a deep cultural trance, unaware of the widespread pathology that has deeply infected us.

We have unleashed a vast devastation on the physical body of Earth. Species are dying at an hourly rate, more than an acre of rain forest is destroyed each minute, and precious, absolutely ir- replaceable topsoil is being washed into the sea, along with tons of pesticides everywhere in the world. We have so damaged the ozone layer of our planet that we now face a deadly threat of global radiation. This is only a small fraction of the immense ruin we are heaping upon ourselves, socially, psychically, and spiritually. And yet, our governments and leaders, our industries and churches con- tinue to act as if these signs of devastation are not the most crucial issues of our lives. We pretend, as we go about business as usual, that someone sometime will solve the problems for us.

As with our personal illnesses, we first have to admit we are suf- fering. This is no small problem, because most of us prefer to re- main *in denial*. When we experience an issue in our family that terrifies us, we try to bury it, and if a family member draws our at- tention to it, we become angry. As we are confronted with the ill- ness of our culture, we again deny it or become angry. But we need instead to name the crisis we live in and learn to respond in a healthy and effective manner. This is the only hope, whether on a personal or planetary level.

Once we have overcome our denial and anger—or skepticism— about the true state of our health, we face a far greater challenge: What can we do about the problem? How do we identify and then change those habits that have caused us to suffer such poor health, so much alienation and pain? There is no simple answer, but there is a place to begin.

We need to discover and embrace a spirituality of Earth, a very practical place where the terrain of our society and the environ- ment converge. That's where we need to begin our cultural healing. We need to open ourselves not only to the crises of our times but also to the precious and stunning beauty of Earth.

Our search is for something deeper than political ideas or ec- onomic policies; it reaches for a new way of life, one that flows out of an awareness of the cosmic story and the sacredness of Earth. We need to learn how to change the habits that have made us so ill culturally and to discontinue the oppressive, addictive, and destructive behaviors we have perpetrated on our planet. In effect, we must liberate the physical Earth, and everything that lives on and in it, from those practices that cause it injury.

This challenge is enormous. Admittedly, it will be hard work and will take generations before we can say we have recovered. But we can and must begin. Then, out of our hope, we can move away from the destructive behaviors of the present. We can say we are *in recovery.*

My experience confirms that the metaphor of illness is indeed a hopeful one. Serious illnesses can be a source of transformation and a doorway to a new life. I have known people with cancer or with AIDS to be sources of hope and to show life's deeper meaning to themselves and others. The symptoms of an illness are the body's primary means of indicating its desire for healing. Our challenge is to respond to the symptoms that Earth exhibits.

When we reverence Earth for its own sake, we create the possibility of prophetic cultural action. We have experienced what happens when the culture fails to understand the reality of Earth's story: It becomes cut off from the people and planet. This cultural death is where we are now, facing the ruin and devastation of the planet. This watershed moment of cultural collapse awakens us to the opportunity for understanding and new health.

There is a new story being told. The new story is about a living universe. We have failed to understand that the universe is alive. The best way to get in touch with the immense notion of a living universe is through story. In this way we come to see that the universe story is, in fact, our story too.

The dynamics of the universe as reflected in the principles of differentiation, interiority, and communion are described in the work of Pierre Teilhard de Chardin and Thomas Berry. These principles will be discussed at length to demonstrate how our cultural life is most vital when we see that each of us, and all that is, is distinct, interconnected, and possesses an interior life.

I will demonstrate how these principles find cultural expression in creativity, compassion, and our capacity to internalize the mystery of the cosmos. From the comprehension of these principles flows a source of energy that moves us into action. Earth becomes the place where these three principles are practiced, where creativity, compassion, and experiences of the depths take place.

A primary expression of our cultural illness is revealed in our struggle with issues of gender. The emergence of the divine feminine and the "green man," a masculine archetype of oneness with the planet, can contribute to the healing of the culture and Earth.

In summary, I take on the challenge of how we are to accomplish the immense task before us. Our hope must draw upon a new understanding of the universe. This understanding provides some insights into how we may fashion a culture for the future and embrace more fully the wisdom of Earth.

Like many others, I have a dream fueled by sacred hope. I believe that relationships help us discover who we are and where we are going, that we develop as people partly through our view of our place in the web connecting us with our ancestors, our teachers, our city, our region, our nation. For many, fortunately, there is a growing awareness of humanity's place in the universe. We can hardly fail to acknowledge that we are at a critical moment in the story of life on Earth. Once-pure water is now unfit to drink; oceans and rain forests are being destroyed; fertile lands are being converted into deserts. Worse, we realize that our children are going to grow up in the world that, having gone to war over oil, is now on the verge of realizing that the petroleum age is over, that the supply of these non-renewable resources is dwindling. As the oil fields burned in the aftermath of the Gulf War, we were reminded of the cost and consequences of unleashing our aggressive behavior on Earth.

We are coming to the close of an era. But this is more than the end of a historical moment; it is the end of a biological period of planet Earth. Life on Earth has the potential to be a beautiful dream or an increasingly violent and chaotic nightmare. But humanity cannot ignore its relationship with Earth. For both to thrive, indeed to survive at all, the dream has to take form.

Exactly what dream can humanity pursue? What are the characteristics of a fruitful relationship with Earth, with the whole cosmos? Let us imagine for a moment a future in harmony with the universe.

This dream throbs with passion and caring on both a personal and a collective level. It is ecologically aware, holistic, and just. Its moral strategy is voluntary simplicity. It is vision-packed, action-packed, and immediate. Propaganda and rampant consumerism are distant, unpleasant memories. The media are accountable and responsible. The dream is loving. We live on Earth in mutually enhancing ways as an expression of a larger sacred community of all life. It is a dream in which we awaken daily to the beauty and sound of the dawn, sunset, mountains, trees, birds, and one another.

In our dream of the future we celebrate the authentic wisdom of all world religions and the movement toward a deep and enduring change in the human heart. There is a reverence for all creation, which is born of awe, wisdom, and "radical amazement."

We reverence the sacredness of our common existence and long to release our collective potential to heal, birth, and transform. We have learned to transcend separateness and fragmentation and to promote planetary survival, and we see ourselves in relationship to the whole of life concerning culture and nature.

We heal any perceived conflict between the need of the person and the requirements of culture and Earth; we affirm the intrinsic value of all of life. We celebrate justice as we move out from our communities to find the many ways that our patterns of living make sense in regard to our history and our origins.

Just as we move beyond ourselves and our communities to become part of the larger world community, we also develop an awakening sensitivity to the story of the universe itself as a sacred story and a primary expression of the divine in all things.

How do we make this dream of the future become a reality? What actions can we take today to ensure that tomorrow will not be a nightmare?

We need to seek liberation, explore our mystical and mythical underpinnings, reject domination in any form, honor quality, seek creativity rather than mere reproduction, reward innovation rather than imitation, promote unity while honoring diversity. In short, we need to live in such a way as to create a world of balance, harmony, and peace. We must in all our decisions reject the petty, the strife-producing, the sensational.

Our dream for the future calls us to a spirituality that reverences and celebrates creation. Our spirituality sees the universe as the manifestation of the divine. We are called to find God in the cosmological order, the scripture of the universe, a scripture that will generate a new language for a new generation. We are at last becoming aware that our story is integral with the story of the universe. Through fully participating in and supporting life by effort, work, pain, and participation, we are able to hope. We need not face the nightmare after all. Rather, we can discover the energies of love.

For Meditation . . .

Manifesto for Freedom and Democracy in Ireland

When children are more valued than bombs
And they read the books that we write
When women are more valued than work
And our homes are no longer prisons
When justice no longer huddles in cells
Nor strangers crouch armed in our streets
When we own our own cities and fields
We will know the meaning of freedom.

Until such time
The cries of our cities and the groans of our land
Will be our songs of wisdom
Our poetry of anger and hope.
Until such time
Our watchful murals and graffitied thoughts
Will be our street newspaper
Our uncensored judgment and art.

But while you dance to our songs
And market our lives
Read our lips:
We are the people of struggle
Ours is the culture of change.[2]

The Unfolding Story

The secret opening through which the in-exhaustible energies of the cosmos pour into human cultural manifestation.

Joseph Campbell[1]

Storytelling

I have always been fascinated with the power of story. Little children love to hear a story before they go to sleep. At camp, people of all ages sit around the campfire at night, listening to and telling stories. In his later years, my father sat on the front porch of our home and invited those who passed by to tell him a story. We know people best when they tell us their story, and we know ourselves better when we reflect on our own.

My Story

I'm a Canadian, the youngest of three children. My family background is Irish-French Canadian. I was raised Catholic in a religiously diverse community and am today striving to be Christian. I have always loved athletics, farms, rivers, and the seasons. Economically we are working-class people, and through the years I have found myself on the side of the oppressed. Living at the end of the second millennium, I am witnessing and participating in enormously significant biological and cultural changes.

I hope by my life to bring attention to the sacredness of all life. I appreciate the beauty of the natural world, particularly as it is manifest in the oceans, rivers, and mountains, in the song of a bird and the voices of the wind and brook. For much of my life I have been reflecting on and responding to certain peak moments in the culture: Vatican Council II, the ecumenical movement, community organization and development, popular education, the human potential movement, depth psychology, projects and approaches to further social and ecological justice and a spirituality of Earth.

Oppression, both internal and structural, holds me back. Internally I feel blocked by fear, the unwillingness to risk, the hesitation that makes possible failure an obstacle to action. I am also hindered by not being able to understand the movements in the culture well enough to act as decisively and confidently as I would like.

I also react to the oppressive structures of the culture. I am distracted by the economic demands of supporting myself. I am frustrated by the need to meet the agenda of institutions that oppose my vision and point of view. I am blocked by the institutional church, which at times stands in the way of the gospel it espouses. I am baffled by a political and a cultural agenda that overlooks the destruction of species and devastation of the biosphere.

The continuing passage of time, which makes each moment more precious and each opportunity more to be cherished, frightens me. I must keep reminding myself that we do not discover our destiny by planning our future, but rather by engaging fully in the present, moment by moment.

Pain has taught me much about what it means to be an outsider. As a child, I felt displaced from my home. This wounded me, but also brought its own healing energy into my life. The physical hardships of childhood have made it possible for me to be drawn toward the poor and the oppressed.

The pathology of a redemption-centered religion has been in some ways a source of abuse. I have experienced this most intensely in the abuse of power and the imposition of an unhealthy sexual morality. Pain has taught me to forgive and let go, to live fully.

I strive to be open to whatever surprises life may offer, to make this short prayer my own:

> For all that has been, thanks.
> For all that will be, yes.[2]

I have always wanted to respond to whatever life would offer me as new or the next step in my journey. I want to be able to say at the end of my life that I have no regrets. I truly want my life to have made a difference, to have influenced others. I also want to face the terror of indecision and doubt. I know that the terror I feel is an invitation, an opportunity to engage fully in expressing my gifts and potential.

I feel that my life has had a certain progression, and that I am in some way on the verge of a next step. I am terrified that I will not recognize that step when it presents itself. The specifics and how it will be different from what I understand now are not clear.

I want to participate in the birth of a new culture, to make a better world for the children, to prepare the way for new life in all its many forms.

The pain of Earth touches me. I feel it in the spread of homelessness, the violent dualism of politics, the possibility of war as sanctioned murder, the devastating loneliness and lack of relationship, especially in our cities; the rampant unemployment and underemployment, the death of species, the abuse of drugs, the poison that permeates the air, water, and land.

I want to take what I have learned and combine it with what I am learning to move it to a new level; I want to take organization, science, education, therapy, and theology and form them into a new relationship with Earth and its peoples. I want to remember that humor, curiosity, gratitude, and love are basic to life. And I want to keep moving toward the future with praise and hope in my heart.

The Role of Story

Story provides a pattern of meaning, coherence, and unity. The story is the primary vehicle for revealing who we are. Human experience is best portrayed as a narrative. A good story rings true, uniting us to what is sacred. It reminds us of our roots and challenges us to consider our destiny. It increases our capacity for reflection and empowers us to engage more fully in life. When we tell or hear a story, two things happen: We are invited inside someone's life, and we also open up to receive the other.

I was part of a gathering at People's Park in Berkeley, California, one evening soon after the student unrest in China's Tiananmen Square. Each of us held a candle and expressed our concern about the violence being unleashed by the government. It was a very moving ritual. But only afterward, as we stood around and told our stories, did we really come to know one another.

As I think about how knowing people's stories often has changed my perception of them, I remember the wisdom of the late Geno Baroni, the founding president of the Center for Urban Ethnic Affairs and former assistant secretary of Housing and Urban Development during the Carter administration. He said that the melting pot of American culture made people "white bread—no crust, no roots, *no story*." He recognized that our story is our identity. Many of his own stories concerned his father and his Italian heritage. He was especially fond of those times when his father would make wine. He would wear white galoshes and jump up and down in a large vat to crush the grapes. I never forgot that story; it revealed Baroni's identity and roots.

Often I will meet people—students, community people, or colleagues—whose behavior may initially puzzle me. Yet after I hear their story, things make sense. And knowing their story helps me to accept them, to understand what they think about themselves, about others, the culture, Earth, and deeply spiritual issues.

Stories are not only helpful, they are essential. Radio announcer and author Paul Harvey ends each broadcast with an anecdote that takes an initial set of circumstances, likely to be interpreted one way, and twists it by revealing what he calls "the rest of the story." As more of the story is revealed, we gain understanding.

Story is a way of entering into another's life. It introduces us to a unique human mystery. It is not a map, which predetermines every detail and eliminates mystery. A compass is a more appropriate metaphor for story: It points out the direction. As people gather and reveal their journey, they are strengthened by the telling and listening. They return to the world wiser, better able to face the challenges of the dominant culture. As storytelling people, our humanity is deepened when we listen to and tell a story. Since we are social creatures, our stories help bring us together and create communion. A story helps us discover for ourselves, as well as share with others, what we value. Recently, a student gave a copy of his story, written for class, to his children for Christmas; it was his way of sharing his spiritual journey with his family.

Stories reveal how we understand our unique relationship to the cosmos, to each other, and to ourselves. Stories about the turning points of our life help us more fully discover our potential. Our stories carry our history, our meaning, our purpose, our roots. We tell stories about our childhood, our family, our culture, the cosmos, and God. In telling stories we remember the past and act our way into a new kind of future. Cultural stories give coherence to our past; they heal and unify us.

In classes and workshops I often invite participants to tell stories. Each time, something important is revealed. People remember a loved one, describe an experience of being in touch with Earth, recount a moment of personal insight. They may tell painful stories of illness, separation, and loss. They may tell stories of ecological devastation and social injustice. Each time, the story brings forth lessons about life and offers guidelines for our spiritual journey.

I remember a man telling about his love for a daughter who was developmentally handicapped. As he told us how much she has taught him and his wife, tears rolled down his cheeks. He felt the pain that physical limitations had placed on the child he loved so much. It was a powerful story. Such stories release a power for life. They can enhance our commitment to a more life-giving relationship with others and with Earth.

A woman from Canada's Maritime Provinces speaks of how surgery for a life-threatening illness melted years of loneliness and restored her vitality and gratitude for life. A lawyer from Ontario recalls a near fatal accident when he was twenty. After nine months in a body cast, he felt reborn. Looking back, he recalls the love of his mother who seldom left his bedside during his recovery. Today he continues her gesture by listening to others. A criminal court judge, he is widely known for his belief in rehabilitation.

A theologian, also from Ontario, relates that spending a sabbatical with his mother during her final illness was perhaps the most important thing he has ever done. Being able to tell her he loved her five minutes before she died strengthened his conviction that each one of us is a unique word that emanates from the heart of the universe. This same man remembers the gifts he received from his handicapped brother. He has learned to appreciate the sacredness of life through his brother's capacity to develop marvelous relationships. These lessons of human worth have encouraged him to spend his energy creating a place where people can flourish.

René Fumoleau, an oblate missionary from France who has spent more than three decades with the Dene people of the Canadian Northwest territories, recounts that when he first came to Canada he introduced the native people to the Christian tradition. As he was about to leave he asked the elders, "What is the most important commandment of the Christian faith?" Their answer was "Never lock your door." Their answer was about hospitality; it is not only good social behavior to provide shelter from the fierce elements of the north, but also important to extend a cosmic hospitality, a welcoming of the mystery of the universe.

Listening to stories and telling them can help us be more attentive to the sacredness of the songbird and the gurgle of a river. As people gather and tell stories with Earth in mind, they are nourished by the beauty of the natural world. A story reveals who we are, what we think of the world, what we believe. Our story becomes the basis for our attitudes, values, and intentions.

I have discovered that by telling cultural stories we are able to find the energy and direction for renewal and change. One example is the story of the Wizard of Oz. At a workshop I invited one person to begin to tell the story and others followed. Each contributed a unique dimension to the story. Then I asked them to reflect on the meaning of this cultural story. Their answers were amazing. They talked about how Dorothy's search for Kansas reflected their own search for roots in their life; how the Tin Man's need for a new heart reflected the heartless world we live in; how the courage of the Lion is required to live in our contemporary culture.

The universe also has a story to tell. It is the story of our origins, the story of how we "were shaped and fired in the same primordial furnace," as Thomas Berry puts it. The universe's story is marked by events such as the emergence of Earth and the solar system (500 million years ago), the first flowering of plants (130 million years ago), and the beginning of humankind (100 thousand years ago). The story of the birth of the cosmos has been told in many ways; one of the most impressive is this poem, "The Creation,"[3] by James Weldon Johnson:

And God stepped out in space
And he looked around and said:
I'm lonely—
I'll make me a world.

And far as the eye of God could see
Darkness covered everything,
Blacker than a hundred midnights
Down in a cypress swamp.

Then God smiled,
And the light broke,
And the darkness rolled up on one side,
And the light stood shining on the other,
And God said: That's good!

Then God reached out and took the light in His hands,
And God rolled the light around in His hands
Until he made the sun;
And He set that sun a-blazing in the heavens.
And the light that was left from making the sun
God gathered it up in a shining ball
And flung it against the darkness,
Spangling the night with the moon and stars.
Then down between
The darkness and the light
He hurled the world;
And God said: That's good!

Then God himself stepped down—
And the sun was on His right hand,
And the moon was on His left;
The stars were clustered about His head,
And Earth was under His feet.
And God walked, and where He trod
His footsteps hollowed the valleys out
And bulged the mountains up.

Then He stopped and looked and saw
That Earth was hot and barren.
So God stepped over to the edge of the world
And He spat out the seven seas—
He batted His eyes, and the lightnings flashed—
He clapped His hands, and the thunders rolled—
And the waters above Earth came down,
The cooling waters came down.

Then the green grass sprouted,
And the little red flowers blossomed,
The pine tree pointed his finger to the sky,
And the oak spread out his arms,
The lakes cuddled down in the hollows of the ground,
And the rivers ran down to the sea;
And God smiled again,

And the rainbow appeared,
And curled itself around His shoulder.

Then God raised His arm and He waved His hand
Over the sea and over the land,
And He said: Bring forth! Bring forth!
And quicker than God could drop His hand,
Fishes and fowls,
And beasts and birds
Swam the rivers and the seas,
Roamed the forests and the woods,
And split the air with their wings,
And God said: That's good!

Then God walked around,
And God looked around
On all that He had made.
He looked at His sun,
And He looked at His moon,
And He looked at His little stars;
He looked on His world
With all its living things,
And God said: I'm lonely still.

Then God sat down—
On the side of a hill where He could think;
By a deep, wide river He sat down;
With His head in His hands,
God thought and thought,
Till He thought: I'll make me a man!

Up from the bed of the river
God scooped the clay;
And by the bank of the river
He kneeled Him down;
And there the great God Almighty
Who lit the sun and fixed it in the sky,
Who flung the stars to the most far corner of the night,

Who rounded Earth in the middle of His hand;
This Great God,
Like a mammy bending over her baby,
Kneeled down in the dust
Toiling over a lump of clay
Till He shaped it in His own image;

Then into it He blew the breath of life,
And man became a living soul.
Amen. Amen.

Liberating Action

At the Institute for Contextual Theology in South Africa, a narrative approach to theology is used to begin to heal the wounds of apartheid. As people tell their stories of racial oppression, they begin to move into action to change a culture of racism. In the barrios of Lima, Peru, at the Institute of Bartolomé de Las Casas, storytelling and listening to the poor are the bases for a liberation theology. In church basements and living rooms in Brooklyn, New York, under the aegis of the Brooklyn Ecumenical Cooperatives, people's stories of their relationship to the land become the energy source that moves them into action to work for affordable housing. As people talk about their ancestors' relationship to the land, they draw on that energy—even though they live in the asphalt jungles of a large urban city.

The pattern remains consistent: Wherever liberating action is happening, stories are being told. Actions emerge in response to stories. Talking to a friend about his work with people who are handicapped, I asked, "How do you get people to respond once they recognize the problem?" He answered, "I just keep inviting them to gather and tell stories." He was convinced that action is the predictable result of storytelling. The strategy for cultural change is telling stories. Storytelling is our most radical approach to organizing.

Stories are inherent in our relationships. They are created out of the connection between a teller and a listener. When two people begin to date, they find that as they become increasingly fond of each other, they want to hear each other's story.

Stories are also told about the place where we were born and where we live. I was touched by the story of a friend who is a rural pastor in Saskatchewan as he told of his love for the prairies. He said that he longs to be home on the prairies whenever he drives east through the Rocky Mountains. His was a story of being connected to Earth.

Stories are a way of reconstructing our consciousness. Stories confirm what we know and challenge us to go beyond. Like the inchworm, stories lead us forward, groping courageously and with curiosity toward the future. Storytelling leads us from perception to decisions formed in hope.

The Universe as Story

My life has been powerfully affected as I have come to understand the universe as story. When we reflect on the sequence of transformational events, we see this great story in four phases: the galactic story, the Earth story, the life story, and the human story. From the origin of the fireball, the birth of hydrogen and helium, the formation of galaxies, planets, and Earth, we are reminded that "we are all made from stardust." This Earth is where life happens, where energy is transformed, where through photosynthesis we are able to convert energy to carbohydrates and oxygen so that plants, animals, fish, birds, and humans can appear and prosper. I am awe-struck to realize that we humans are that dimension of this story whereby the universe emerges into awareness of itself. I see that I cannot know myself or my culture apart from the unfolding of the universe. Through telling Earth's story, I have come to realize that I am deeply interconnected in a common evolutionary adventure.

We tell this story of the universe in science, visual art, poetry, music, and now in our spirituality. All the creatures of Earth also tell it: Birds sing and wolves howl. In the beauty of a tree's branches and leaves, or in rivers with clear running water the story is told. All of us, every creature on Earth, are privileged to listen to and tell this cosmic story.

Personal stories evoke a connection to the root of our being. They communicate episodes and transformations in our lives. Our culture too has a story to tell. The story of the Hebrews told in Scripture is one familiar cultural story. Our challenge is to see our story, our culture's story, and the universe's story as a sacred story.

What does the universe's story reveal? What do we learn as we walk through a garden at night and look at the sky and see the stars? What is the lesson for us when we understand that we breathe the same molecules that Moses and Jesus breathed? What does it mean to be a child of the fireball? What can we learn from the universe and Earth about being engaged in life when we stand on a mountain, listen to a spring, or see the beauty of a flower? How do we understand from the universe the need to be totally committed? How does Earth teach us to be fully present to the others in our life?

The response to these questions is found in science, art, and spirituality; we are all interconnected within the universe. We are the universe and the universe is us; we intimately embrace the world and the cosmos. The universe is a personal place.

The Universe as Source of Revelation

There are three basic patterns in the universe: differentiation, subjectivity or interiority, and communion. *Differentiation* refers to the uniqueness woven into the universe. Every snowflake, every person is different. To comprehend each rock, flower, bird, or human is to see how it is different from the others. The cultural metaphor of the melting pot does not fit here; the image of a mosaic is much more appropriate.

> . . . Each is different from the other, a particular experience of beauty. Everything has something to give that nothing else can give. Each creature is a unique manifestation of the divine, with a special gift and responsibility. . . .

Interiority means that the universe is made up of subjects, each possessing a capacity for deep interior experience. This interior experience releases energy to organize and sustain patterns of relationship in a specific way. Interiority refers to the configuration of the Milky Way, to the way geese fly in formation, and to human interaction manifest in the self or a cultural form such as education or government.

. . . We have a capacity for deep inner experience, for interior depths. Everything carries within it the deep mystery of its capacity for existence and experience of the divine. From this place we recognize and express our inner voice. Our culture needs to find its voice and listen with a deep sensitivity to the voices of each member of Earth community. Only when we awaken to listen to the brook, the bird, and the migrant in the barrio will we cease to plunder and destroy. . . .

Communion implies relationship. Scientifically it is based on a gravitational interaction. Communion teaches us that seemingly discrete entities are also interconnected and bonded into a pattern of togetherness with all that is. Similarly, communion culturally extends to us the opportunity to belong, while differentiation challenges us to retain our own uniqueness.

. . . We are bonded into a pattern of togetherness with all that is. We have a capacity for relationship, a gravitational attraction that must extend from ourselves to other humans, to the natural world, to all that is. Only so will life on this planet survive, flourish, and be permeated with compassion. . . .

The Cosmos and the Trinity
The universe is not a one-time event, but a continuous moment-by-moment diffusion of goodness into all of life. The universe, Earth, and the culture are constantly developing. They are involved in a process that is alive.

God is not some kind of remote mechanic tending a static universe. God is alive and evolutionary, an imminent mystery that permeates all of life. We are bathed in a God who is pure act. This understanding is rooted in our tradition and in the cosmic story. It fashions an incarnational evolutionary theology.

Our relationship to the divine is mediated through storytelling. Narratives that are personal, cultural, and cosmic heal the pain of distance, separation, and meaninglessness, and bring about a heartfelt connection with self, other, Earth, universe, and the divine.

The mystery of the Trinity is at the heart of the Christian tradition. The Trinity reveals to us that the very heart of oneness (God) is a community of equality and diversity. There is a direct connection between the dynamic patterns of the universe (differentiation, communion, and interiority) and the Trinity.

When we reflect on the Trinity from this perspective, we see that the Creator (Father) expresses the principle of differentiation. We are reminded that each dimension of the universe, each act of creation, is an expression of uniqueness. As we turn our attention to the different manifestations of existence, we become aware of the enormous diversity that flows from the creator God. The Word (Son) reflects interiority. The self-organized activity that flows from the Word is manifest in the configuration of the stars, the structure of a rock, or the relationship entered into by a group of people. In each case the Word provides a pattern of activity that reveals meaning, purpose, and depth. The Word is the origin, the source, the place from which story comes, the locus of divine revelation. The Transformer (Holy Spirit) provides the energy that holds things together. This principle of communion helps provide an understanding of ultimate purpose through relatedness.

These constitutive patterns embody the principles of the universe and are integral to the dynamics of the Trinity. When our life moves according to these principles and dynamics, it is approaching our dream of a new culture and new Earth. A culture developed in this way will enhance the unfolding of the universe and deepen our experience of wisdom and mystery. When communion, differentiation, and interiority are present, not only is the culture reborn but the divine is palpable and present in trinitarian form. We can assert, then, that the rebirth of culture is more about relationship than rules, more about connectedness than accomplishment. It is both fluid and fixed, a quilted tapestry that is both distinct and one.

The culture needs the universe story, Earth story, for us to tell our own story. As we listen to one another's stories we become informed, share joy, relieve pain, awaken our imagination, and provide a web of memories and relationships. Stories quench our thirst for meaning and connectedness; kneaded together, they become the food that nourishes us for our journey. Thomas Berry's words capture this vision: "We bear the universe in our beings as the universe bears us in its being. The two have a total presence to each other and to that deeper mystery out of which both the universe and ourselves have emerged."[4]

The following story of the universe is a context for all our stories, those told and those yet to be told.

> Imagine that our 15 billion year history was compressed into a single calendar year. . . . The Milky Way galaxy self-organized in late February, our solar system emerged from the elemental stardust of an exploded supernova in early September, the planetary oceans formed in late September, the Earth awakened into life in early October, sex was invented in late November, the dinosaurs lived for a few days in early December, flowering plants burst upon the scene with a dazzling array of color in mid-December, and the universe began reflecting consciously through the human, with choice and free will, less than ten minutes before midnight on December 31st![5]

Or, as Elie Wiesel succinctly stated—and this applies to cosmic, cultural, and personal stories: "Whoever survives a test, whatever it may be, must tell the story." That is our task.

For Meditation . . .

Our destiny can be understood . . . only in the context of the great story of the universe. All peoples derive their understanding of themselves by their account of how the universe came into being in the beginning, how it came to be as it is, and the role of the human in history. . . . Shocked by the devastation we have caused, we are awakening to the wonder of a universe never before seen in quite the same manner. No one ever before could tell in such lyric language the story of the primordial flaring forth of the universe at the beginning, the shaping of the immense number of stars gathered into galaxies, the collapse of the first generation of stars to create . . . the formation of Earth with its seas and atmosphere and the

continents crashing and rifting as they move over the atmosphere, the awakening of life.[6]

This connectedness of our own life processes with the dynamics of an all-embracing universe.[7]

Questions for Discussion and Reflection

1. Story is a primary vehicle for human intelligibility. What in
your story reveals your ancestors' relationship to Earth? What were
the values, vision, and struggle they brought to this relationship?
What implications do you see for your life today?

2. The unfolding universe can be understood as story. What is
the sequence of transformational events that constitute the universe
story?

3. What are the three principles, patterns, or tendencies of the
universe? How do they provide a compass for our work of cultural
renewal?

4. How do these three principles of the universe constitute a renewed understanding of the Trinity?

5. What stories have you heard, told, and lived that have altered
your consciousness and connected you to the sacredness of life?

6. To celebrate the unfolding story, take a piece of yarn or cord
and arrange it in the form of a spiral in the center of the room. Place
a candle and marker at the center and at intervals along the spiral
indicating the major phases in the story. Participants go into the
spiral and light the candles in sequence announcing the particular
moment in time. In conclusion, each participant takes the "cosmic
walk" from the center. When they come to the end, they proclaim,
"The universe celebrates (name)."[8]

Creativity and Uniqueness

Every creator painfully experiences the chasm between his inner vision and its ultimate expression.

Isaac Bashevis Singer[1]

Appreciating Diversity

The Rainbow Coalition under the leadership of Jesse Jackson celebrates the beauty of ethnic differences. Jackson often says, "Red, yellow, black or white, we are all precious in God's sight"; that is, each of us is unique because we are created that way. Diversity is at the heart of the universe and is a result of its creative process. Said another way, creativity is the art form of the universe.

We are slowly beginning to appreciate differences of gender and race. It is time—and past time—to respect the gifts of women, minority groups, and other oppressed peoples. Much more needs to be done to halt oppression and challenge stereotypes.

We can celebrate the diversity in the unique beauty of the places where we live. I have lived in California for a number of years, and I have grown to savor the rugged majesty of the Sierras, the timeless rolling of the tide of the Pacific Ocean, the stateliness of the redwoods, and the beauty of the Golden Gate.

As a native of southwestern Ontario, I also appreciate the vitality of the rivers, the rich black soil that is the womb for corn, sugar beets, and lima beans, and the rugged grace of the maple tree. At the center of this appreciation for differences is a realization that each expression of creation is itself unique and beautiful. Each piece of land, each body of water, each person is without repetition and inspires wonder. Earth, as the expression of all these nuances of beauty, is our teacher in the great school of creativity. When we begin to comprehend that each expression of the cosmos is an expression of the divine and that every creation is unique, we begin to grasp the meaning of difference and creativity. Creativity thrives in this deep appreciation of differences.

Moments of Cosmic Surprise

Creativity can be viewed as the continuing expression of the fireball, a cosmic unfolding. This dynamic event makes variety possible in the universe. Each unique act of creation is a continuation of the single energetic event stretched out over the past fifteen billion years.

My own reflections on creativity have raised many questions. For me, creativity is expressed in the deeply rooted urge to give birth, to pass something on, to let go so that an image, idea, or project can be born and experienced by others. It is a process by which I discover my own uniqueness and appreciate anew the varied ways of being of others. Creativity is spontaneous, free, and surprising.

For example, when a meeting, a class, or a community project "falls together," there is magic and imagination in the air. I remember a workshop several years ago in St. Paul, Minnesota. At the end of the evening, people began to sing and celebrate. In just a few minutes the entire gathering was on the stage singing and dancing. Everyone was moving in response to the music, yet everyone was dancing in his or her own way. This was not a planned event, but clearly a creative outburst. This moment simply came, and we were all surprised. Something was born within and around us that we had not planned. Each person released energy to this event. We let go, and as we surrendered to the process, something was born. I learned from this that creativity is not only an individual event but a collaborative effort as well. Sometimes workshops—and other projects—take on a momentum of their own, and sometimes they do not. I can lead the workshop, but I can't bring the outpouring of creativity into being.

Creativity in the culture flows from a deep appreciation and respect for diversity; at the same time, the creative process itself reveals more completely our own uniqueness. The work of Teilhard de Chardin speaks to me about creativity: "The future is more beautiful than all the pasts."[2] Creativity is about being drawn forward, allured, enchanted by a passion, a desire and fascination for beauty. When a person is enchanted by the desire to play music, paint, build an organization, or teach a class, creative surprises occur. Something erupts from the depths and everything shifts. There is an experience of being carried forward and embraced by the energy of the universe.

Creativity as an expression and path to uniqueness also involves struggle. When I write, I struggle to put on paper what is on my mind and in my imagination. Part of my writing involves being vulnerable by revealing my thoughts and feelings to others. I have to struggle to escape from abstraction and become open to people. Dr. Jean Shinoda Bolen describes creativity as similar to the attitude of a woman about to give birth: She unconditionally surrenders to whatever happens.

Another dimension of the creative process is that it is ongoing. I learned in community organization that one issue eventually leads to another, and another, and so on. A neighborhood project involving a parking problem leads to a landlord issue and then to a housing committee. Creativity involves being flexible enough to follow the dynamic as the process unfolds. The results of creativity are not linear or predictable, but rather full of surprises.

We can also view creativity as a theology of resurrection. The creative process involves being born again, and again. A seed dying to give birth to a plant is a profound expression of death and resurrection. This paschal dynamic of dying and rising is woven powerfully into the fabric of life. We see it whenever something full of life is generated from emptiness, when alienation is replaced by relatedness. When we quit trying to control life and rise to its surprises, we are involved in creativity. From the perspective of a spirituality of Earth, resurrection and creativity apply to the whole Earth, which continually is being reborn as it participates in the great act of creativity.

Appropriate "letting go" is a difficult part of the process. A friend told me about going to a seminar on using time given by a day-planner company. As she tells it, the central message of the several hours of class was that jotting down every activity, every moment of the day, every phone number, every interaction in a notebook would somehow guarantee control of life. As the participants left the meeting, the leader asked my friend what she thought of the process. She responded that it had taken her fifty years to relinquish the illusion that she could control her life and she didn't intend to take it up again. She had realized over the years that harmony with the life forces around her was more important than ephemeral notions of control. She felt she was just beginning to live her life creatively.

The Sacred Impulse

As the years go by, we increasingly feel the need to give birth, to pass something on. We pursue outlets for the generative energy that draws us forward into procreation. For me, writing is one way of giving expression to this; community development is another. Some things we begin because we think we have to. For example, Friends and Advocates, a project in Toronto that works toward building supportive relationships between former mental patients and community people, is now in its second decade; the Regional Connectors Project, now grown to include over three hundred individuals and groups, provides information and support to people interested in creation spirituality.

These are responses to my deep-seated desire to leave something behind. The projects that we birth are expressions of our creativity. We do not own them, and often they surprise us. Like parents with their children, we give them life, we give them love, and we give them wings. It is then that these projects take on the characteristics of true creativity; they become uniquely their own. As Kahlil Gibran wrote:

> Your children are not your children.
> They are the sons and daughters of Life's longing for itself.
> They come through you but not from you,
> And though they are with you yet they belong not to you.[3]

Stifling Creativity

Creativity has not been espoused by bureaucratic institutions, nor has it been a part of school curricula; creativity is, in fact, unwelcome in the structures of the dominant culture. Schools, corporations, and governments are interested in predictable behavior, not in the surging chaos of the unexpected. Doctors, lawyers, and clergy are schooled for uniformity. Each profession has a process of initiation that ensures predictable behavior and conformity (law clerks become lawyers, interns become doctors, and so forth).

It is common practice for organizations to violate uniqueness in the name of treating everyone the same. This rationale for sameness violates differences and promotes injustice. The rich receive tax breaks when grouped with the poor and middle class. Ethnic differences are blurred in the name of nationalism.

In the creative process we do not really know what to do next; we simply surrender any control and become astonished as we celebrate what happens. In this process of unleashing the wildness of our imaginations into the culture, we celebrate rebirth and remain untamed.

The rebirth of culture we hope and work for must celebrate differences. It must have a reverence for the differences of resources, ethos, language, and history. Not every task is suitable for every person. I find factory work, for example, to be very repetitive, with little outlet for creativity. When I was in high school I worked at a pressure cooker factory, performing the same task each day, completing five hundred units each shift. Weeks later, when it was time to return to school, I felt that a deadness had descended on my spirit. I wonder now, as I did then, how men and women endure this work for years on end. While it is true that repetitive acts can become a mantra or a spiritual practice, the factory is clearly not that for many people. At least, it wasn't for me!

Much of the work performed in our culture is drenched in conformity, which promotes boredom and burnout. The people who perform these jobs year in and year out pay an enormous spiritual price. The creative process, on the other hand, can be an instrument for inspiration, joy, and even healing. When a friend of mine began to write, she soon left her sick bed. In fact, she completed an entire manuscript in a few weeks. The forces of creativity are so powerful that they need to be channeled but not repressed. When this happens, we can become healed and whole.

Creativity on the human level is a particular expression of beauty, a manifestation of our unique gifts and responsibility. Creativity is engaging in the evolutionary process of Earth; it is participating in the divine act of creating the cosmos. It is an epiphany in which each of us gives expression to the unique microcosms that are our life. The adventure of creativity fashions our world of experience into tabernacles of mystery and depth. As a child brings home pictures from school to adorn the refrigerator, we would do well to find forms in poetry, movement, and images for the ongoing expressions that are taking place in our souls. By honoring our imaginations and caring for our creativity, we engage in soul work and make our lives more meaningful and open to rapture and surprise.

We celebrate the ongoing event of the incarnation, manifest in each act of creativity and uniqueness that flows from the Creator God. We participate also in each moment of newness and surprise that erupts in us from the divine. This adventure of incarnation and resurrection enfolds us in the divine expressions of uniqueness, creativity, and surprise.

What to Create?

Perhaps the most meaningful question we can ask another person, or ourselves, is this: What do you want to create? This question speaks to our deepest dimension. Creativity is not about comparison or competition; it is about being called to give birth to something uniquely our own, to give our gift.

Creativity is the energy of the divine in motion in and through our imaginations and lives. It is an expression of the maternal impulse that lies in each of us, woman or man. It can find expression in a relationship, a project, a work of art. It can give birth to a new culture.

Creativity speaks to us about the purpose and destiny of our lives. It reminds us to be passionate and determined to do something without which we would be only half alive. It confronts us with hard choices; we have to die to one thing in order to rise to something else. We cannot go to South America and remain in North America; we cannot, at the same time, go to the library and go to the mall.

For many years I felt I could choose any and all options. But as the years went by I realized that it was necessary to do *something* rather than *everything*. I saw that my life had been permeated with the "lazy-susan" syndrome: I sampled a bit of everything. We must instead choose what we most want to create. Many people go through life without being clear about this. When we can say, "I want to do this, not that," the doorway to creativity opens and energy flows. But we must choose. In the silence of our hearts we must contact the creative impulse and give expression to ideas and efforts that we previously failed to recognize or understand. This connects us to the creativity of Earth. Then we can answer the question of what contribution we want to make to Earth and what we are willing to risk to do so.

The dynamic of creativity involves both creating the creator as well as creating the work of art. In playing the music, the musician is changed. We can't paint a picture without also transforming the landscape of our soul. We cannot stand outside the act of our own creativity; the organizer and the organization undergo the same profound change.

Waves of Cultural Creativity

Cultures have certain waves that crest and fall. They are expressions or outbursts of the creative process. In the early and mid-1960s we experienced the waves of Vatican Council II. With its signature document proclaiming the church in the modern world, many Catholics felt new energy and hope. The false dualism between sacred and secular had been dissolved. The windows were opened to bring fresh air to institutionalized decay. By the late 1960s and early 1970s, another cultural wave had come to the fore. With race riots from Newark to Watts and peace marches in protest of the Vietnam War, a cultural response to the urban crisis and an unjust war had been born. Soon I found myself involved in urban training and community organization in Toronto and Chicago.

In the 1970s and 1980s a new burst of cultural energy was manifest in the churches through the birth of the ecumenical movement. I became engaged in theological education in Toronto at Canada's largest theological school. As the infrastructure of the culture eroded, a large group of people began looking more deeply for meaning and purpose in life. By the mid-1980s I became caught up in the ascending crest of a renewed interest in spirituality. I extended my interest in social justice to encompass a concern for Earth. Each of these events in my life was a manifestation and a response to cultural creativity.

As I think again about these creative moments in the culture, I realize how much energy and new life they provided. Each moment makes available a particular expression of cultural creativity. These waves in the culture are an invitation; they provide an opportunity to join with others who are also drawn forward by similar energy. Reflecting on these creative moments in the culture has altered my understanding of the creative process. I have come to see it as a collective process; that is, each of us responds *in our own way* to a particular moment in the culture that we experience *in common*.

Mystics and Psychology

Creativity happens in the psyche when our consciousness moves from being human-centered to creation-centered. This act of creativity is like a resurrection of the psyche. It makes mysticism possible and rescues us from an anthropocentric world view. Otto Rank, a colleague of Freud, writes, "When religion lost the cosmos, [humankind] became neurotic and invented psychology."[4] These prophetic words shed light on my own experience in therapy. I learned that psychology, like the rest of the culture, can be burdened by a redemption-centered consciousness. It can place the human at the center of the universe and reinforce a preoccupation with being healed.

The problem is that we tend to want to be healed and then healed some more. This springs from a distorted theology that constantly reminds us of a need for redemption. This preoccupation with healing reveals a deep-seated conviction that there is something indelibly wrong with us. Our neurotic pursuit of perfection grows out of a sense that we are fatally flawed. The dominant cultural understanding suggests that personal healing must precede and be completed before social engagement can follow. But there is no evidence that psychological healing prepares one for political activity. Both are important; they need to happen simultaneously.

The psychology that Rank says has "lost the cosmos" tends to shrink our world and make it small. In this world, therapy is an endless pursuit.

Dr. Stanislav Grof, the prophetic psychiatrist and author of *The Holotropic Mind*, sees the psyche as co-extensive with the universe. The context for healing becomes the cosmos and not the person. We understand that we are in the cosmos and cosmos is in us. The psyche is not an object to be probed and analyzed; rather, it is a source of wonder, sacredness, and celebration.

Resurrection happens in the psyche when we move from a preoccupation with self to an awareness of the cosmos. In this act of resurrection we celebrate the psyche's capacity to heal itself from fragmentation within and alienation without. When we trust the psyche to heal itself, we will also trust the processes by which we achieve this goal.

Experiencing Creativity and Uniqueness

Artists name their creative activity in intuitive language. Author D.H. Lawrence talks about "that spark that flies into consciousness . . . a little creative change." Artist Kenzi Myazawa writes, "We must forge our own beauty; we must set free the greyness of our labor with the art of our lives." Musician Miles Davis says, "I'll play it first and tell you about it later." Dancer Martha Graham, responding to an inquiry about her performance, comments, "I don't know. If I did, I wouldn't have done it." M. C. Richards, poet, painter, and potter, talks about her work this way: "The words bubble up and speak for themselves." Canadian artist Loren Harris states, "I strive to get to the summit of my soul and point from there where the universe sings." Psychiatrist Stanislav Grof describes creativity as "agony and ecstasy and the fusion of both." Saul Alinsky, community organizer, acknowledges the need for creativity in cultural change: "The organizer is driven by a desire to create." And Brazilian educator Paulo Friere writes: "Education is an act of creation, unlocking other creative acts, a process from the inside out."

In the act of creativity we are most fully human and most fully divine. The process extends to Earth and the cosmos. Martha Graham captures the meaning of creativity:

There is a vitality, a life-force, an energy, a quickening which is translated through you into action, and because there is only one of you in all time, this expression is unique. And if you block it, it will mean that through any other medium—the world will not have it.

For Meditation . . .
To be an artist means not to complete or count; it means to ripen on the tree, which does not force its sap, but stands unshaken in the storm of spring with no fear that the summer does not follow. It will come regardless. But it comes only to those who live as though eternity stretches before them, carefree, silent and endless. I learn it daily, learn it with many poems, for which I am grateful. Patience is all![5]

Questions for Reflection and Discussion

1. How does the principle of differentiation shape and focus your understanding of creativity?

2. Why is the question "What do you want to create?" so important at this moment in history? What is your response to this question?

3. How does resurrection deepen your understanding of creativity?

4. Many would say that burn-out, boredom, and violence are the results of repressed creativity. How does your experience affirm or deny this statement?

5. Creativity is unwelcome in the structures of the dominant culture (corporations, governments, churches, and schools). What evidence do you have to substantiate this statement?

6. How has the practice of creativity contributed to your life and to the culture? In what ways has it enhanced your comprehension of your destiny and call?

Interiority and Depth

A being's unique interiority, depth, spontaneity, and creativity present the creative unfolding and ultimate mystery of the cosmos.

Charlene Spretnak[1]

To be with children and witness the power of their imaginations is fascinating. Their rich inner life is revealed in their eagerness to dramatize among family and friends highly imaginative depictions of animals. Often their images are funny, sad, wonderful, and deeply entertaining. Children speak as if their dream life is still part of the waking reality. As adults, we have often lost this language for our inner life.

Still, as other expressions of creation, we carry the capacity to express our voice to the entire Earth community, to be fully present and sensitive to every other being, to acknowledge the sacred depths that reside in each of us. From the recesses of our being we can express gratitude for fond memories and for events that have touched our heart. These experiences enhance our awareness of our inner depths; they dissolve disillusionment, emptiness, and yearning into a celebration of meaning, depth, and relatedness with ourselves, others, and the divine.

I often ask friends, "What are you thinking?" The question is prompted by my need to have access to their interior depths. This is where we have our reservoirs of inexhaustible energies. These energies are a powerful source for bringing about the birth of the new culture that is our dream. Our immediate challenge is to awaken our interior sensitivities to experience more fully the beauty, mystery, darkness, and dynamic balance of Earth. From these recesses of human self-awareness will flow the organization and action to heal the wounds of Earth and the people of Earth.

Our artistic expression also flows from our inner life. Van Gogh's sunflower and Michelangelo's *Pietà* came from this source. We draw from this same place in our acts of creativity. Our art may not be expressed in painting or sculpture, but may be the creative acts of raising a family, fashioning friendships, or offering support and solitude to those in need. We become artists of compassion at the birth of a child, through a rich, active dream life, in healthy and passionate personal interaction. Psychologist Jean Shinoda Bolen writes, "When knowledge of this myth dimension comes into your possession, it can help you find your bearings and a path that is true for you, one which reflects who you authentically are."

Many of the things I have pursued over the years were motivated by a desire to understand my inner life more fully. I entered

therapy, spiritual direction, cultural work, and sometimes friendship for this purpose. I was striving, often unknowingly, to make
conscious the story, the myth that lived within me. I have come to
understand that knowing my own story and discovering my own
myth is an important part of becoming a new person in a culture in
the throes of a paradigm shift.

One way of talking about the new myth for our time is to say
that our goal is to make it possible for the story of Earth to be the
story of our culture on Earth. The myth, the story of this new relationship with Earth, makes the energies of the cosmos available in
cultural form; interiority and depths are important dimensions of
Earth story.

Internalizing the Mystery

When scientists discovered evidence of the origin of the universe,
they said that these seeds of the cosmic fireball were like the "foot-
prints" of God. When we connect to the deepest recesses of our interior life, we also find ourselves in touch with the divine. A friend
said, "When I go into the ravine to participate in the restoration of
the creek, flowers, and trees, I know that I am healing a dimension
of myself that if ignored and left alone would become much like
that neglected field." A wise woman of years said to me that
throughout her life she had seen a blade of grass as a manifestation
of the divine. "In response to the sun and rain it becomes green and
tall in the spring; it is a sign of the resurrection. It is of Earth as we
are; it has deep, strong roots that reach into Earth."

These women, like many other people, have a cellular relationship with Earth. Each sees her true self as a dimension of
Earth, as an ecological self. They see Earth as not mine but me.
They see healing as a personal, social, and planetary event, a bal-
ancing of the inner and the outer from the place where we experience an interconnectedness with Earth.

Thomas Merton was fond of saying that he never felt more connected with his brother monks in the monastery than when he was
"alone in solitude." We are interconnected and in communion with
the natural world. From this perspective our questions become
Who am I? and What am I becoming? We must decide that before
we can address the next question, What am I going to do? As one

woman said, "Maybe I can't save the rain forest, but I can save the tree in my backyard." By seeing ourselves as a dimension of Earth, we see more and more how the poor of Earth—the homeless, those marginalized by sexual orientation, income, race, mental illness, and other forms of oppression—are themselves connected with the suffering of the poor Earth.

With an increased sense of urgency and sensitivity, we hear the confirming voice of a small child who demonstrates the unconditional love with which he has been raised. He is fond of saying what could be held as a mantra for our work of cultural rebirth: "Mother Earth holds us all the time." It is for him and all the children that our efforts make sense.

The awareness of this new story of Earth resides within the depths of the human psyche and within the entire Earth community. Just as there are galaxies in the cosmos and trees, birds, and oceans on Earth, so also our interior life is a realm of incredible vastness. Carl Jung speaks of this: "When you look inside yourself, you see the universe and all its stars in all their infinity . . . an infinite mystery within yourself as great as the one without."[2] In our deep inner knowing, we are liberated from an introspective consciousness. We view our interior life from the perspective of the cosmos, not the confines of our human experience.

As we live with Earth, so also in a very real way Earth lives within us. Our lives are nourished by the internalized mystery of beauty. When we feel the power of the ocean, the tenacity of a mountain lion, the tenderness of a child, and the wisdom of an older person, we have been touched by the beauty of our living Earth. In the "grand canyons" and "galactic constellations" of our interior life we are nourished by the waterways of wisdom, the memory of blue skies, the power of the magnificent trees of courage, the serenity of a gentle breeze, and the strength of rich, dark soil.

When we internalize our experience of the mystery of Earth, we undergo a "psychic photosynthesis." Photosynthesis transforms and incarnates the energy of the remote sun. In psychic photosynthesis we ingest and make the mystery of the cosmos part of our life. We not only consume Earth, but our psychic inner life is shaped by Earth in ways that are deeply mysterious. In fact, we incarnate Earth in our hearts and minds. We have a deep mystical connection with Earth. We become open and vulnerable to what Earth is saying to us. Earth's story gives expression to the meaning and purpose of our lives. We learn to listen more fully to our inner voice, a voice that speaks to us through the seas, the sky, and the trees. We experience a renewed sense of the sacred and the mystery that lives within us.

We reverence in a new way the unique manner in which life is offered to us. The sciences tell us that every creature is unique. This is also true of every moment; none can be repeated. Mystics have told us that life is a series of unrepeatable moments, each one charged with a uniqueness that has not been there before and will never be again.

Our stories and our experience of Earth give us new energy by which to live more fully and imaginatively. As we fashion new images, rituals, and behavior to transform our environment, we create a new constellation of feelings and beliefs. In our ritual-making and storytelling we create hope for a new culture. Charlene Spretnak writes of this new culture as "a human construction inclusive of creative tensions and reflective of our embeddedness in the Earth body."[3]

Culture is an extension of Earth, not something superimposed upon it; myth and story narrate an unfolding from within. They capture an experience of sacred mystery. When we portray these narratives in ritual fashion, we create an experience of how the patterns of the cosmos can be inculturated.

Self-Organization

As a young child I was fascinated by my uncle who could blow smoke rings when smoking his pipe. I was entranced as the smoke obeyed some inner urging that caused it to form rings in mid-air. When I was older, I watched the Canada geese fly south for the winter from the shores of the St. Claire River. Each time I was amazed by the precise configuration of their flight paths. The manner in which human relationships emerge is even more remarkable.

One day in a classroom I was teaching the paschal mystery. When I completed the section on the spirituality of the cross, I realized that the class needed to express its feelings but seemed uncertain about how to do it. I put on the song "Hallelujah, the Great

Storm Is Over." Everyone in the room stood up and started dancing. A new configuration of relationships had come into the room
spontaneously. Some couples began to dance; then they began to
cluster into groups; then they formed even larger groups. After a
while they formed into a long line of people dancing together.

This phenomenon of self-organization is universal; it can happen
during a conversation, after a meal when something special has occurred, between two people attending a baseball or football game,
in a classroom, at a community meeting, at a ritual. It can happen
anywhere. Fritjof Capra writes, "A living organism is a self-
organizing system. . . . Its order in structure and function is not imposed by the environment but is established by the system itself."[4]
This capacity for self-organization and self-renewal is found in the
dynamics of the universe. Thomas Berry writes in *Befriending the
Earth*, "The universe is not a puppet show but a reality functioning
from within its own spontaneity."[5]

Our privileged role as cultural workers is to make available and
find ways for the self-organizing dynamic of the universe, this
"creative energy" that continually bubbles up from Earth and within ourselves, to express itself more fully in new processes, structures, and potentialities. One way of evoking this energy is to invite
people to tell their stories, to listen to what is deepest in their
hearts, to create ritual and art. The energy that erupts from these in-
teractions will provide the basis and direction for the new culture.

At a workshop I invited people to recall and share their memories of being "at one with Earth." A young man told us how he
climbed to the top of a mountain in Hawaii and made the loudest
sound he could. In doing this, he said, he felt close to God. As he
told his story, I could hear the energy in his voice and his deep appreciation for Earth. As people expressed their memories, something important was happening. From the spontaneous energy that
was released, a new structure, a new set of relationships was born.
The results were not planned; they were self-organized.

This dynamic of spontaneity emerges from the deep recesses of
our interior life. It flies in the face of the conformity that is so embedded in many structures. Self-organization is not about sameness. It is rather about honoring the spontaneity that emerges from
the deep wells of the interior life of Earth and the people of Earth.

This gathering of energy into action from the place of our deepest experience can contribute to the healing of Earth. The courageous task of the new human is to provide for future generations by entering into a deeper and deeper rapport with the natural world. As cosmic people, our privilege and responsibility is to guide the destiny of planet Earth. As we take up the task of cultural rebirth, we expand our capacity to accept, protect, and foster the welfare of Earth. In the canyons of our interior existence we contact the divine, gain access to the Word, and become new people who recognize our oneness with the universe.

As people gather to tell stories and reflect on their feelings, new structures form. These structures demonstrate the dynamics of the universe; they have within them the elements of communion, differentiation, and interiority. The rituals that bring these about can involve music and movement, drumming, readings, group processes, processions, blessing.

Ritual, art, and story make connections between our actions and our consciousness; we connect our actions to the great story and to the presence of the divine; we act in more transformative ways. Ritual, art, and story can make the world better, more just, and more whole. As we see our lives in words, images, and music, our hopes are raised and we become energized. When a group of us gathered to plan an Earth Day liturgy, we called forth and honored the sacredness of Earth through dance, song, and mask-making.

Creating Ritual

Rainer Maria Rilke revealed a profound truth when he wrote that "words are the last resort for what lies deep within." He was reminding us that the non-linear language of symbol, image, and metaphor is a more appropriate vehicle for revealing the deeper truths of our lives. This communication will be enhanced by silence, movement, art, and music. The ritual that unfolds becomes a bridge between the stories of our lives and the actions we engage in. When we give ritual expression to the themes that are generated from our stories, we celebrate the experience of our common existence. These celebrations contain enormous power; what is signified in the symbol is also brought about in the culture. A ritual of unity not only expresses oneness, but it also transforms our relationship into an experience of oneness.

Creating ritual is about empowerment and experimentation; it is most profound when done in the context of ancient forms such as processions, eucharist, chants, and music. Ritual enhances the meaning and focus of our lives by marking the change of seasons, feast days, and important events in the life of a community. These events are most meaningful when they are simple and contain elements of spontaneity. Ritual helps build community by providing connections among participants and the traditions to which they belong. We can create rituals about gender, body, Earth, cycles of nature, the seasons of the year, and the universe story.

One example of a ritual that contributes to fashioning new symbols for the culture is simple yet insight-producing. Participants gather in a circle and are given balls of different colored yarn. As they throw the balls to others in the circle, the yarn forms a web and is multicolored (differentiation) and interconnected (communion). The power in such a ritual is that it opens people to insight. As they look into the web they have created, they can speak more easily of the matters of the heart. One person may mention her fascination with the experience of snow, and another how wisdom and pain have been his teachers. As people express their thoughts and feelings, they reveal their interior life.

Eating together is one of the most basic ritual forms. When meals are combined with procession, movements, chants, songs, symbols, and stories, we are able to internalize mystery and celebrate the deeper truths of our lives. On a Good Friday recently, a group gathered to name the way the crucifixion is happening now. We remembered the rain forest, abused women, endangered species, racism, AIDS patients, hunger, addiction, pollution. In the ritual that followed, we mourned these crucifixions of Earth and its peoples.

On another occasion I invited group members to choose which of the three principles—differentiation, communion, or interiority—they would like to celebrate. The differentiation group spoke in the languages of their ancestors and celebrated their diversity. The communion group dramatized a meal in which they could feed each other while being unable to feed themselves. The interiority group told of a blind man who listened to a tour guide describe the Grand Canyon and repeated over and over, "Isn't it beautiful? Isn't it beautiful?"

Simple ritual can celebrate the dynamics of the universe and also invite us into a deeper experience of the divine through our awareness of the presence of the Creator, Word, and Spirit. Ritual becomes a vehicle for healing by internalizing the mystery of the universe and God.

As we take our vision and apply it to the forms of the culture—education, politics, economics, psychology—we will honor our interior life, develop intimate relationships with Earth, and become new people.

As we engage in dialogue with Earth, we are healed from displacement, from being cultural refugees whose vision is denied, voice silenced, and desire for connectedness opposed. Seeing ourselves as a species among species, we come home to Earth—to animals, plants, rocks, cosmos, and people.

The reinvention of humanity will flow from the experiences in the recesses of their being. People will not be alone; they will feel connected to their deeper self with an experience of strength and courage; they will be at one with themselves and with Earth. There will be a sense of peace and purpose in their lives. They will neither regret the past nor fear the future. Their imaginations will expand. In friendship, loss, and love, the new humans will celebrate themselves as that place where the universe comes to self-awareness while remaining connected to every expression of the natural world. At one with the recess of their being, they will live with an experience of abundance and strength, nurtured by beauty and filled with gratitude. Victor Hugo captured this notion when he wrote: "There is one spectacle grander than the sea, that is the sky; there is one spectacle grander than the sky, that is the interior of the soul."

For Meditation . . .
I went down into my inmost self, to the deep abyss whence I

feel dimly that my power of action emanates. But as I moved further and further away from the conventional certainties by which social life is superficially illuminated, I became aware that I was losing contact with myself. At each step of descent a new person was disclosed within me of whose name I was no longer sure and who no longer obeyed me. And when I had to stop my exploration because the path faded beneath my steps, I found a bottomless abyss at my feet, and out of it came . . . arising I know not from where . . . the current which I dare to call my life.[6]

Questions for Reflection and Discussion

1. "When you look inside yourself, you see the universe and all its stars in all their infinity . . . an infinite mystery within, as great as the one without. . . ." How do you understand this statement of Carl Jung?

2. How does the splitting of the atom and the discovery of energy and space in subatomic particles contribute to your understanding of interiority and depth?

3. Fritjof Capra suggests that self-organization happens when "order, structure and function is not imposed by the environment but is established by the system itself." What experiences have you had that confirm this principle of self-organization?

4. How does ritual provide a vehicle to express "what lies deep within"? Through reflecting on your experience of good ritual, name the components that are necessary to bring it about.

5. Compose a poem, painting, or ritual to give expression through word, image, or symbol to the landscape of your soul.

Communion and Compassion

Relationship is the essence of existence.

Thomas Berry
Brian Swimme[1]

Questions about justice and compassion have been the most engaging and sometimes the most puzzling of any I have attempted to address in my life. On occasion I have asked myself whether my Irish heritage, widely known for being anti-government and resilient in the face of oppression, has contributed to my impulse to work for the underdog, to be on the side of the poor. Whatever the reason, I have always found myself aligned with the marginalized and disadvantaged. Recently, two issues have captured my energy and attention: working to stop a foreign policy that displaces the people of Latin America, and confronting fast-food chains that rape the forests to provide pasture for cattle, destined to be slaughtered and sold for hamburgers. When the Latin American bishops proposed that the work of theology is to be done from a "preferential option for the poor," they made a monumental contribution to the work of liberation and justice. Whatever the personal reasons for doing this work, the ecological devastation in our day has convinced me that the option for the poor needs to be extended to poor Earth. An environmental wasteland has given a new meaning to poverty.

I have noticed that although compassion is the litmus test and culminating touchstone of a spirituality of Earth, it is often misunderstood and neglected. It has frequently been my experience that justice is not well understood in relationship to the new way of seeing the world.

Not only are we troubled by the pain of social and ecological injustice, but we are also troubled by the approaches taken to heal injustice. Our approaches to social justice have remained embedded in the distortion of a redemption-centered culture. Many who become engaged in work for justice burn out and leave the work, very discouraged. Guilt and a misguided obligation have parched their spirit and contracted their vision. On occasion, marriages and personal health have been sacrificed on the altar of community concerns. Once I was asked to encourage a man to run for the presidency at our community convention. His marriage was breaking up; something was wrong. The work for justice had become itself an act of injustice. Much justice work also has overlooked the interior life. Justice workers often do not feel nourished in their efforts to liberate the oppressed.

Friends and colleagues have often reported that their efforts toward social justice have left them fragmented and alienated. Given this experience, they retreated. But work for justice can be different. The work of compassion can be an adventure in communion. It can best be understood in relationship to the universe as an "intimate presence" and a response to the "supreme challenge" of extending love and relationship to self, others, and Earth.

I remember an event that marked the beginnings of my organizing experience. My older brother was the best pitcher on our baseball team. I wasn't playing much, so he and I convinced our manager that I should catch when my brother pitched. This was my first organizing project, my first experience of being involved in shifting patterns of relationship to achieve a desired result.

Later, as a student with the Industrial Areas Foundation Saul Alinsky Training Institute, I became excited about the opportunity of learning more about how to empower the poor and disadvantaged. Remembering how I solved the problem of not playing enough on my local baseball team, I applied what I had learned to my justice work. I looked for others with whom to play the game of justice: people with influence, to whom I could listen, and with whom I could work.

My experience in community organization was liberating. In Toronto a delegation of community people went to City Hall to meet with the commissioner of public works who had consistently refused to cooperate with neighborhood people. Residents were outraged at the number of tickets they were getting for parking on the streets near their homes. They wanted to organize to obtain affordable permits for overnight parking. When the leader of our delegation presented our concerns and received the commissioner's promise to come to a community meeting, the people felt excited and empowered. This experience was a great gift. It is one of my fondest memories from my days of community organization. The people felt, perhaps for the first time, that they had influence over their lives.

I recall a story that appeared in a neighborhood newspaper the day after our community convention in Chicago. It began, "In the American Revolution, this time in Chicago's Southwest side, the Mayor (Boss) replaces the monarch as the object of dissent and the throne has moved to the fifth floor of City Hall (Mayor's Office), but the reason for dissent remains the same—repugnant taxation." This organizing project was a reenactment of the vision and spirit upon which the country had been founded. To be involved in this revolutionary work was exciting, empowering, and fun, yet some questions remained unanswered. I was troubled by what seemed more like *in*version than *con*version. I saw the "have-nots" become the "haves." I saw people achieve the ability to act. This was very rewarding. Their actions achieved a solution to the issues they had identified. I was still new in the work, but it was clear that something was lacking. I was concerned that there seemed to be no corresponding interior change. There was an exchange of power, yet no deeper change. Since then, I have learned that the power of domination can be transformed to an ability to act fully from within and among the entire Earth community. How to effect this change was my quest. Later I would hear from Alinsky that there can be no true revolution (structural change) without an accompanying reformation (internal change).

I understood the principle but was troubled when I saw communities at one time alive for change later becoming racist and opposing the very things that had brought their organizing efforts into existence in the first place. A classic example is the Back of the Yards project in Chicago's packing house district, the neighborhood where Alinsky did his first major piece of work by bringing justice to the world of industrial workers. Today it is an embarrassingly racist community. This troubled me then, and it troubles me now. The Back of the Yards project was a significant example of local democracy. People achieved political freedom in an industrial neighborhood. Great things were accomplished as relationships were fostered and built. The organizing worked. What went wrong?

Despite having organized my baseball team and having worked as an organizer in Southwest Chicago and the Riverdale and West Central communities of Toronto, there was still something missing. I was grateful for the legacy of Alinsky and his colleagues. I deeply believed that the first act of justice-making is organization. I realized that organization is a way to get things done, a way of changing systems and, I hoped, changing hearts. However, I was still searching for increased wisdom about justice-making. What I was searching for, I now understand, was the meaning of compassion.

While puzzling over these questions, I inaugurated a project called the Institute for Communities in Canada at Humber College in northwest Toronto. I invited to the institute a team of men and women who were at the time working with Paulo Freire and the Institute for Cultural Action. Freire, the Brazilian educator, had been exiled from Brazil and later from Chile for his educational methods. Instinctively I felt that his work would provide answers to my questions. His conviction that we need to liberate the oppressor as well as the oppressed (outlined in his book, *The Pedagogy of the Oppressed*) was a new insight for me; it changed my understanding of justice. ". . .trusting the people is the indispensable precondition for revolutionary change. A real humanist can be identified more by his trust in the people, which engages him in their struggle than by a thousand actions in their favour, without that trust."[2] This insight collapsed the dualism implicit in a "have-have not" mentality. I read Freire's book and traveled to Cornwall-on-Hudson, New York, to meet his colleagues Sally Timmel and Ann Hope, who had returned from work in Africa.

Both Alinsky and Freire articulated a four-phase approach to their work. The phases converge in unexpected ways. Their manner is different, but their intention is very much the same.

The Dynamics of Compassion

Phase I. Both Alinsky and Freire begin with an initial stage of storytelling. They invite people to talk about their experiences and their hopes for a more just world. The initial storytelling provides the grounding. It assists people to envision their world in a different way. People clarify their vision when they hear what others have to say. The story gathers energy and provides an opportunity to experience unity. For Alinsky, this is the *pre-organizing* phase. For Freire, it is the *descriptive* phase. In each case, people are invited to tell their story and express their vision. This invariably generates a sense of hope. I was often told that "you organize with your ears." It is very true.

Phase II. The second phase focuses on the pain, obstacles, and structures that perpetuate injustice. For Alinsky, this is the *dis-*

organizing phase. It involves letting go of structures and dismantling systems that cause injustice. It involves shaking things up to form new patterns and relationships, new capacities to act.

For Freire, this second phase involves *codification*, naming the oppression. He means identifying the internal obstacles and structural blocks that take away internal freedom and the capacity to make external choices. For the people of Brazil, the external block was the military regime; for us today, it may be employment policies and the internal obstacle of fear.

Phase III. The third phase is about moving toward something new. For Alinsky, the *organizing* phase is about creating organizational forms for those who have no representation. Alinsky was fond of saying that "the organizer is driven by a desire to create." The organizer's work is to create organizations around issues for which there is no organizational response. For example, if a neighborhood has small children and working mothers, an organization to provide day care is needed. Another need may be an after-school program for children whose parents are still at work when they get out of school.

Freire also saw his work as a context for creativity. For him, education is the way we express creativity. The action that results is something we create. It flows from us, teaches us, and ultimately transforms us. This is the phase of *cultural action*. He writes, "Education is an act of creation, capable of unleashing other creative acts, a process from the inside out."

Phase IV. Both Alinsky and Freire view their work as bringing things to a collective whole. For Alinsky, compassion and justice are accomplished through community organization by bringing the community together to develop a community of action. The old structures that are at the service of justice are combined with the newly organized ones. Together, they cooperate in the work of transformation. The old and the new structures are woven together into a fabric for justice-making. This mass-based (involving the whole community) organization becomes the vehicle for resolving issues and working toward justice. This is the *reorganizing* phase. Whether expressed in a town hall meeting, a union gathering, or even a political convention, something exciting happens when people gather to express their collective energy for justice.

For Freire, the process of transforming the culture happens through *conscientization*. He writes: "We cannot create knowledge without acting. The focus of the action is to transform the world." It is here that compassion happens. In conscientization, critical reflection for the sake of transformation occurs and people and structures are changed.

The Quest for Communion and Compassion

Despite my years working with Alinsky and Freire and their colleagues, and feeling the power and effectiveness of their work, I felt something was still missing. I continued to feel the need to see justice and compassion in a new way.

Within the universe there is a comprehensive bonding, a compassionate embrace that brings everything into relationship with everything else. This mysterious energy celebrates mutual relatedness and heals alienation. This pattern toward a cosmic communion finds expression in the tapestry of an interconnected culture. It makes possible a relatedness of everything to everything else and is far beyond our previous capacity to imagine.

As we courageously open our hearts to the pain of our planet, which we experience as our own, we respond to the impulse to participate in the healing properties of our living Earth. As instruments of communion and compassion, we become present with love and kindness to envelop the entire Earth community in an experience of mutual belonging.

When I discovered this spirituality of Earth, I began to view justice in a new way. It was a spirituality that extended itself into the natural world. Earth itself became a source, participant, and model for justice-making. I began to see that justice takes place when we have relationships of intimacy and equality, that justice can be experienced as communion and compassion.

Communion is not a private undertaking, but the central fabric of all our lives, a privilege and opportunity. Through communion and compassion we participate in an event that is already occurring. Thomas Merton speaks of this when he addresses his fellow monks: "My dear brothers, we are already one. But we imagine that we are not. And what we have to discover is our original unity. What we have to be is what we already are." Earth is an instrument of compassion; here we find relationships of balance, harmony, and peace.

Compassion is what Earth is and does. Suddenly, the sense of being part of a community of compassion made sense to me. It is the cultural expression for communion, the energy of inter-connectedness that is alive in the universe. Compassion is about experiencing communion, about bonding and extending our capacity for relationship. I had read Meister Eckhart's words, "The person who understands what I have to say about justice understands everything I have to say."[3] I began to see more fully what he meant.

Compassion is woven into the fabric of life. It is not inversion or competition; it is a relationship, an experience of communion. It is who we are and what Earth is and does. As Earth is coded for compassion, so are we. The words of the civil rights anthem—"We Shall Overcome . . . We'll walk hand in hand, We shall live in peace"[4]—made new and even more sense to me. Compassion is about relationship, connectedness, and the energy that draws us together in love. Martin Luther King, Jr., eloquently articulated this view when he said, "In a real sense all life is interrelated. All [people] are caught in an inescapable network of mutuality, tied in a single garment of destiny."

Compassion adds a new dimension to justice-making. Justice-making is not a human desire for rearranging properties and re-aligning power, as important as they are. Earth is constantly creating compassion. Flowers are blooming, rivers are flowing, photosynthesis continues happening. As humans, we are invited to remove the social and ecological obstacles that destroy Earth's creativity and be courageous as artists of our own lives. For too long, justice has been seen as a mechanical realignment of power and money that I was taught it was. Suddenly, I realized that Earth was a living, interconnected system. Our role as humans is to participate in this communion of relationships. Participation in the system of Earth can contribute to harmony and balance; it can be an experience and expression of compassion. It points invariably toward justice for the entire Earth community.

At this time in history, many institutions of our culture are ailing; they are not participating in compassion. In fact, their collapse is creating a self-absorbed and unhappy people. Earth is telling us something we need to hear. The annihilation of species and re-sources and the nuclear threat of planetary destruction reveal the enormous need we have for a new perspective on justice. Compassion with regard for Earth is our agenda for today and our hope for tomorrow.

Just as I had learned that the psyche has properties for healing, I discovered Earth as resilient, self-healing, and an archetype for communion and compassion. As I reflected on the cycle of the seasons and that night follows day, how the sun, water, and Earth give life to the pear tree that provides food for the hungry, I celebrated the powerful healing dynamics of Earth and began to examine more fully the meaning of cultural rebirth.

In the dynamics of compassion there is a shifting from being human-centered to being Earth-centered. The Earth becomes our teacher. We celebrate and acknowledge the way in which newness and life are infused into every drop of water, the vitality in every grain of sand, the divine goodness reflected in a gentle breeze.

Compassion and communion also draw us to a deeper appreciation of the pain and oppression that is imposed on our planet. We feel connected to the poor in Guatemala and to the rain forest in Brazil. Out of the cosmic crucifixion of Earth, creativity and newness abound. As we participate in the planet's creativity, we become what Hildegard of Bingen calls a "flowering orchard." Perhaps the most important task of our time is to fashion a web of relationship to heal separation and promote interdependence, to bring about compassion in the culture.

In evoking the abundant creativity of Earth, we notice in a new way what compassion is; we become instruments of inter-connectedness. To create compassion is to support the healing properties of Earth. Compassion happens when we listen to the anawim. When we recognize the wisdom of the voiceless, we are celebrating compassion. Compassion becomes an expression of cultural therapy that will bring healing to people, plants, rivers, and wildlife.

In the work of compassion there is no separation between the personal and the planetary; there is a direct connection between the crack in the ozone layer and the crack that is sold in the streets. There is an indelible connection between social injustice and ecological devastation. The relationship between the destruction by cocaine and the destruction of the atmosphere by hydrocarbons is one act. We belong to the universe; each part contains the whole.

Compassion is about extending our capacity for relationship toward both the atmosphere and the street. Cultural rebirth will happen when there is relationship and relatedness. When alienation is transformed into community, isolation into uniqueness, when people feel honored for who they are, when they are listened to, healing will happen. When images, stories, and myths express communion and compassion, the culture will be born anew.

It is my experience that institutional bureaucrats often do not want to meet with people about whom they have to make decisions. Repeatedly, when they meet people and develop a relationship, they act differently. They become more compassionate. In a similar way, ecological justice will blossom when the bureaucrats, and all people, are closer to the natural world. If we walk on Earth and are touched by the beauty of a flower, the rhapsody of a bird's song, and the delicious gurgle of a brook, we treat Earth with reverence. When we celebrate the sacredness of Earth and see there the God who is in all things, we truly have a basis for compassion. We will then know Earth as our spiritual home, a place of revelation where communion is experienced and made known.

Compassion is a sacred, intimate relationship; it is love. To act justly is to create loving communion with a spouse, the ocean, a tree. In our communion-compassion-lovemaking we are also unique.

When we extend our love for a person and a place into the classroom, the board room, the bedroom, the legislature, and nature, we are engaged in compassion. As we fall in love and internalize the mystery of relatedness, we extend our embrace to all of Earth. In our approach to compassion we move from a human-centered abstraction to bringing the challenge of relatedness to new structures with new hearts that love all creation.

I have come to see Earth as the only viable context for compassion. The work of communion and compassion supports the harmony and balance that is already woven into Earth. It supports the self-healing properties of Earth. As we remove the illusion of separateness, we learn from Earth about love; we experience communion and relatedness. The "book of nature" reveals to us that Earth is our sacred home, a place where balance and harmony exist. Communion and compassion, then, are both an awareness of the interconnectedness (consciousness) and a determination to bring them about where they are not yet present.

Communion and compassion heal the aneurysms, the ruptures in creation, through participating in the creation of a bonding that is intimate and full. Compassion is at the heart of the Christian tradition. It is not a specialty for a significant minority. It is about relationships, love, celebration, and a reverence for Earth.

A spirituality of Earth will relieve our work of compassion from too much purpose and too many whys. It is about being, about participating in the divine creative energy that will heal Earth and render our planet whole.

Our invitation is to experience compassion, to fall in love with ourself, with each other, with Earth and the cosmos, to become vulnerable, open, and connected.

To practice communion and compassion is to stop putting poison in our bodies or burying toxins in the ground, and to support ecological practices such as reforestation, which purifies the soil, air, and water.

There is a direct relationship between our destiny and doing compassion. Meister Eckhart wrote, "If you want to discover who you are, do justice." Compassion, the full engagement in life, provides a window of opportunity into the next step in our life. By engaging fully in the culture to change it, we achieve a new understanding and appreciation of the universe and the dynamic patterns that reveal its deeper meaning.

Myth-Making

The journey into compassion is a journey into fashioning a new myth. A myth is how we make sense out of what appears to be a senseless world. Myths give meaning to self and to community, tell us where we come from, where we are headed, and what is possible and appropriate. We need myths and depend on them daily. We particularly need myths that support the transformation of the culture and connect this process to the dynamics of Earth.

The myth that is being born in our time is the way we understand our relationship to the planet. In the middle of this century Sir Fred Hughes wrote: "Once a photograph of Earth taken from the outside is available—a new idea that is as powerful as any in history will be let loose." We now have that photograph and it is the seed of a new myth. By exploring the heavens we can achieve a new planetary ethic and a new raison d'etre for the people of Earth. Communion and compassion become our goals. This photograph brings home to us that killing for apartheid makes no sense, that war in the Middle East becomes even more untenable, that the liberation of men and women is a mandate. The photograph of Earth from the outside has become, in a new way, a basis for healing separation and promoting our participation in an holistic universe.

For Meditation . . .

The edge of the sea is a strange and beautiful place. All through the long history of Earth it has been an area of unrest where waves have broken heavily against the land, where tides have pressed forward over the continents, receded, and then returned. For no two successive days is the shore line precisely the same. . . .[5]

The shore is an ancient world, for as long as there has been an earth and sea there has been this place of the meeting of land and water. Yet it is a world that keeps alive the sense of continuing creation and of the relentless drive of life. Each time that I enter it, I gain some new awareness of its beauty and its deeper meanings, sensing that intricate fabric of life by which one creature is linked with another, and each with its surroundings.[6]

Questions for Reflection and Discussion

1. How does Earth's expression of harmony, balance, and peace contribute to your understanding of compassion as an extension of your capacity for relationship with the entire Earth community?

2. How do you understand compassion as being about both reformation and revolution in which the oppressor and the oppressed are liberated? How does celebration enhance our understanding of justice-making and compassion?

3. How do the dynamics of compassion as outlined in the work of Saul Alinsky and Paulo Freire provide a framework for your efforts in justice-making? Have you experienced some approaches to justice to be themselves unjust?

4. "If you understand what Earth has to say about justice, you understand everything it has to say." What is your understanding of this adaptation of the words of Meister Eckhart?

5. How do you understand how the work of compassion has been altered or enhanced as a result of seeing Earth through a photograph from outer space?

The Rebirth of Culture

The world today is on the verge of a new age and a new culture.

Bede Griffiths[1]

A Society of Goodness

The source and energy of our dream for a cultural rebirth can be found in a theology of the incarnation. Rather than a single historical event two thousand years ago, we can view the incarnation as a continuing diffusion of goodness into all of life, including our relationships with ourselves and our loved ones, our political and public life, and especially our relationship with the entire Earth community. The divine presence is everywhere; Bethlehem is our home today.

The reality of the incarnation is capable of transforming our culture by bringing new life to it. It points to the ultimate destiny of the world—the new culture and new Earth of our age-old vision. As a place of divine mystery and a source of revelation, Earth is filled with infinite possibilities for new life. Yet, if we fail to embrace this incarnational reality, if we don't view the world as being continually impregnated with new life—sacramental and interconnected—then we are in danger of seeing our culture as determined and Earth as dead and distant.

The work of cultural rebirth is to generate stories and myths that will enhance humanity's relationships with the natural living world around us. Animals are genetically coded to act in particular ways: Ants live in colonies, dogs form packs, and so forth. We also have tendencies to act in particular ways as a result of genetic coding: to live in community, to govern ourselves politically, to express our thoughts and images through the arts to create our culture. The specific expression of these genetic tendencies is greatly influenced by the stories and myths that are deeply configured in our collective unconscious.

Our myths and stories can guide and inspire more healing ways of living on the planet. They can greatly contribute as we fashion the rebirth of culture. As we discover new myths to live by, we will be able to reverse our resistance to the natural world and work in unity with it. For example, people often deny the weather patterns and geography of their region. Rather than plant grass in the desert, we need to celebrate the beauty of cactus and sand; rather than deny the seasons, we need to learn to appreciate the heat and the cold. As we become open to the pain that is part of the natural world, we can invent new modes of living and new ways of celebrating and being intimate with the sacredness of the entire Earth community.

This vision of Earth as a sacred and living place gives us a new way of seeing our culture and encourages us to ask a primary question: Where do we begin the work of revitalizing our culture? In other words, where can we find Bethlehem today, the unfolding of the incarnation in our time, as we move into the twenty-first century? Such a place is needed for us to find allies, resources, and encouragement. Without the support of others who share a similar vision, we risk failure, disappointment, and possibly despair. Yet because the culture has such a sacred and generative dimension, we know that the divine continues to break through and become incarnate in different ways and places.

Cultural Workers

There are also obstacles that block the rebirth of culture. Saul Alinsky proposed that the primary obstacle faced by those working in the field of community organization is mass resignation. He argued that communities need an effectively articulated and hope-filled communal vision to sustain their work. Without such a vision, once their work is confronted with the predictable resistance that all change produces, workers are very likely to despair. A sense of fruitlessness can weaken resolve and undermine ongoing efforts. On the other hand, efforts rooted in a vision and properly supported can transcend inevitable discouragement.

Paulo Freire says we resist cultural change because we don't see the problem or because we believe the problem is so large that nothing can be done. One geographical group of people, for example, may dismiss acid rain as a problem that affects other parts of the world. They don't see it as a problem for them. Urban dwellers, to cite an example of the attitude of inevitability, usually see industrial pollution, such as smog, as an unavoidable consequence of city living. Freire points out that before we can undertake any effective, let alone transformative, action, we need to see clearly what is really going on. We need to be aware of the nature of our culture's organization in terms of who is affected by specific relationships and who benefits by them. Through creative action, which should flow naturally from our new awareness, our *con-*

scientization, we can begin to transform the culture and ourselves.

The rebirth of culture is central to our life on planet Earth. We have the power to shape the present moment while envisioning a future that is fresh and transformed. It is our dream, a story that is happening but is not ended. The future is a vision to be lived, whispered, written, and announced in songs, poems, and art all over the world.

Robert Bellah, sociologist and author, calls culture those "habits of the heart" that find expression in various ways, especially through image, art, customs, values, beliefs, social structures, and story. Culture, to Bellah, is those patterns of meaning that any group or society uses to interpret and evaluate itself and its situation.

A Cultural Renaissance

We who live in this renaissance time, this time of new birth, need to use our gifts in extraordinary ways. We need to direct our energies toward reclaiming the original purpose and pattern of our existence. By exploring new patterns we connect more deeply to our meaning, purpose, and destiny.

In the medieval period, Chartres Cathedral was an architectural expression of cultural rebirth. It gave expression to a new understanding of the relationship among the divine, Earth, and its peoples. Chartres was intended to be a lasting statement of belief in the sacredness and unity in the natural world.

The new Chartres that we must create for today will not be a building; rather it will be a story fashioned from a constellation of relationships. But it, too, will articulate the existence of the deep union we all share with Earth. And as this understanding is embraced by our culture, it will bring us to increased reverence for both the human and non-human communities. Because this story will champion Earth values, it will bring together the needs of people and those of the planet.

But where will the new Chartres be built? Where will we begin our work of cultural rebirth? One answer must be where we see the best and the worst of our problems: in our schools. We need new types of schools to help us reflect critically on our society so that we can see it clearly and effectively begin the work of its transformation. Today, millions of our children are rejecting what they are being offered in place of a true education. Instinctively, our children know their schooling does not meet their deepest needs, that it not only fails to prepare them for today, but that it seems unaware of the challenges awaiting them tomorrow. Rather than socialize people into failing systems, our schools need to become "new cathedrals" for the work of cultural rebirth.

Jean Houston, author of *The Possible Human* and childhood friend of Teilhard de Chardin, conducts "mystery" schools in Colorado and New York. By awakening her students' imaginations, she explores with them the relationship between their culture and their spiritual needs. Once they come to see and feel the contradictions of their old culture, her students make concrete changes that reflect the kind of world they want to live in. One, as we saw, who could not save rain forests by herself, promised to care for the trees at her home. A young man voiced a desire to work with people with AIDS. Yet another spoke of her decision to "get off the fast track" and find work that was socially and ecologically meaningful. Others spoke of renewing their marriages, working with the poor, finding time for reflection that would guide them to the next phase of their journey. New images and the beginnings of a revitalized culture emerged from their discernment.

A colleague who has studied with Houston once asked group participants to write of their hopes and images for a new culture. Then she invited a smaller group to dramatize some of the images. The responses were full of energy and hope. Such are the beginning steps toward fashioning a new culture.

To move toward a rebirth of culture also requires that we pay attention to the profound beauty of the natural world. Our creative lives depend on it. What we know in our hearts to be sacred and beautiful we have learned from the splendor of the natural world. Barry Lopez, writer and naturalist, says that when we debase the landscape "we stand to lose our sense of dignity, of compassion, even our sense of what we call God."

The natural world and the sacred are inextricably linked. In the thirteenth century, Meister Eckhart wrote that to appreciate the beauty of nature we needed to understand that our own natural beauty holds a sacred meaning: "Every creature is full of God and is a book about God."[2] Only when we behold each creature of Earth as a manifestation of the divine can we move beyond the present into the hope of the future.

Liberation Through Cultural Action

Movements such as liberation theology begin where people are oppressed and where there is a deeply felt collective pain. Ralph Waldo Emerson advised us that pain provides meaning and challenges us to make sense of the mystery of life and make ourselves stronger and more courageous. He writes: "They have seen but half the universe who have not been shown the house of pain."[3] The pain of oppression directs us to what deserves liberation. From the broader perspective of the planet, the challenge of freedom from oppression is extended to the natural world and is expressed as a preferential option for Earth.

Liberation theologian Leonardo Boff addresses cultural change in terms of what he calls *ecclesiogenesis*, or a rebirth of the church. To form a church where people understand one another, where they are creative, trusting, loving, and loved, Boff says, calls for a radical change from below and outside the established structures. In Latin America, church base communities—small Christian communities —have become the primary instrument for cultural change. In such communities the disenfranchised have come to believe that they have the power and responsibility to shape the way they see each other and the world in which they live. What these people have created is a place, a "cathedral," where they gather, share, and tell their stories. Then, guided by the wisdom of the group, they engage in community action to form a new society, to put flesh on their dream. Applied to the larger culture, this approach promises a new vision that will activate a zest for adventure and foster the flame of hope.

Many people in North America are forming groups to do such work. People in recovery, women, the poor, those seeking a spirituality of Earth are examples of various base groups in our culture. Yet these groups need to take on a new dimension. As Thomas Berry states, we need to move beyond the idea of democracy to "biocracy." In his view, the idea of democracy is exclusive in regard to Earth and hence shares a complicity in its destruction. "In our political thinking, then, we must go beyond democracy to biocracy. Above all, we need to go to the Earth, to the natural world, as the source whence we come and ask for guidance."[4] A world view that sees Earth as dead or inert will only lead to greater domination and more death.

Freire sees the primary barrier to renewal as a "culture of silence," or what others may call a "conspiracy of silence." Frankly, we must awaken from our lack of awareness, from our inaction and despair. When we discover our authentic voice as a fully conscious people, the voice that speaks for us with power and authority, we come to know who we are. As we learn to know and trust our own experience, we can come together, tell stories, celebrate, heal, eat, and act in common. It is the certainty of our voices that will move us from being mystified (separated) to being mystical (connected).

Looking at the World Through the Incarnation

This experience of universal connection or oneness (mysticism) is central to our work. The starting point of our work, the basis for our solidarity, is the understanding and belief that our mystical union with nature will dissolve our separation and connect us with self, Earth, the people of Earth, the cosmos, and the divine. When we accept this cosmological challenge to align ourselves with the oneness of the universe, we invite the experience and power of mysticism. The grounding of mysticism permits us to overcome the persistent and false sense that we are somehow unconnected, not just from Earth but from one another.

We do not all begin with the same expectations or resources. A participant in one of my classes expressed with great power and energy the darkness and hope he saw in a world that has already experienced the incarnation:

Looking at the world through the window of the incarnation, I see that each time that the word has been made flesh it has been obscured and hidden, disoriented and distorted because the subtlety with which the divine has been eradicated from our planet is insidious.

I see nations increasingly being divided by their long suppressed differences. I do, however, see some small pockets of those who seek another way, who refuse the lies, refuse the violence; and then I see even smaller pockets of those willing to pay the price that their consciousness calls them to.

Looking though the window of incarnation,
I see
the rebirth of culture
beginning in our midst.

For Meditation . . .
Society must be transformed by a new type of social responsibility, a new humanity appropriate to a new Earth.[5]

The path spirituality takes is a path away from the superficial into the depths, away from the outer person into the inner person, away from the privatized and individualistic into the deeply communitarian.[6]

Questions for Reflection and Discussion
1. How is your response to the question "Where is Bethlehem today?" a statement about cultural renewal? How does your response reflect your understanding of the Incarnation?

2. Mass resignation, inertia, and mystified consciousness are primary obstacles to the hope for a rebirth of culture. Reflect on this statement in the light of your experience.

3. Complete the following statement: Looking at the world through the windows of the incarnation, I see . . .

4. How do you understand cultural rebirth as a genesis happening from within, below, and outside existing structures?

5. How is the rebirth of culture a celebration of the sacred and the liberation from political and personal oppression?

News from Planet Earth

Things as we know them are falling apart. There's an unease across the country today. People know that something is wrong. . . . War is only a symptom of something much deeper. Poor people have long known what is wrong. Now the alley garbage, the crowding and the unhappiness and the crises have spread beyond the ghetto and a whole society is coming to realize that it must drastically change its course.

Earth Day 1970[1]

The Dark Night of Our Cultural Soul

We live in a culture where chasms divide us from ourselves, from each other, from Earth, the universe, and the divine. As we discussed in earlier chapters, the principal manifestation of this fragmentation is that more and more people experience a lack of story, a sense of their roots. We need to invent new myths, new images, new symbols, and new language. For example, the symbolic melting pot of sameness must give way to a new symbol: the rainbow of diversity. The societal urge to destroy or ignore differences illustrates an illness that infects the soul of our culture.

The violence that is unleashed on minorities in North American cities confirms this cultural pathology. We are destroying the cities of this continent by propagating violence, crime, and death. Soon exhausted petroleum resources will devastate our transportation systems and energy supply.

Dissatisfaction with this culture of death and accelerated change is seeping into our consciousness at all levels. In *Generation X: Tales for an Accelerated Culture,* Canadian author Douglas Coupland portrays people born in the late 1950s and 1960s as longing for permanence, love, and home in a culture unable to respond to their needs. They experience life as demanding their total energy yet promising little in terms of deep satisfaction. Many have taken dead-end jobs and retreated from their expectations and dreams.

The collapsing infrastructure of the culture inoculates people with a permanent wanderlust. We are a people on the move, hoping to find an idealized sense of community in the next town, the next job, or the next relationship. We are propelled by emptiness, anger, and fear. We are overwhelmed by a tremendous devastation that seems to dwarf our capacity for constructive behavior and drain our hope.

This moment has been characterized by *Time* magazine as a process of "fraying" or "a culture of discontent." These metaphors for the dominant culture name this decade as the time of a society "obsessed with therapies and filled with distrust of formal politics." These metaphors also confirm that the dream of growth and prosperity has failed. Industrialization and production are *not* the answers to those who search for meaning. Progress has proven to be an inadequate panacea.

Movies, novels, and other art forms strive to capture the pain, grief, anger, loss, and desire that reside within a culture that is migrating in stumbling steps from the melting pot of sameness to the mosaic that celebrates differences in unity. The family has become an embattled paradise—a target for advertising demographics, a taxed corporation rather than a locus of love, and all too often a place of violence, where women and children suffer abuse that dehumanizes them and shrivels their souls.

We are experiencing the dark night of our cultural soul. The United States is among all nations first in military spending (almost one billion dollars a day), ninth in illiteracy, tenth in longevity, and seventeenth in infant mortality. "A nation that continues to spend more on programs of national defense than on programs that uplift is a nation nearing spiritual death," said Dr. Martin Luther King, Jr.[2]

Destruction surrounds us. The human cost of greed is a billion people living in poverty and 250,000 children dying of starvation *every single week*. The regional and economic disparity, so prevalent on our planet, is powerfully portrayed in the following reflection:

If the world were a global village of 100 people, one-third of them would be rich or of moderate income, two-thirds would be poor. Of the 100 residents, 47 would be unable to read, and only one would have a college education. About 35 would be suffering from hunger and malnutrition; at least half would be homeless or living in substandard housing. Of the 100 people, 6 of them would be Americans. These 6 would have over a third of the village's entire income, and the other 94 would subsist on the other two-thirds. How could the wealthy 6 live in peace with their neighbors? Surely they would be driven to arm themselves against the other 94 . . . perhaps even to spend, as Americans do, about twice as much per person on military defense as the total income of two-thirds of the villagers.[3]

The ecological devastation of Chernobyl, Bhopal, the Middle East, and Prince William Sound is beyond calculation.

In our large urban centers an undeclared war of cocaine addiction, social hatred, confined housing, homelessness, and unemployment is being waged every day. The daily litany of bias attacks and hate crimes—murders, rapes, suicides, and drive-by shootings—testifies to the deep cultural pathology that affects our cities.

The very guardians of order, the police, have been infected with our cultural love affair with violence. Millions watched the 1991 videotape of the Rodney King beating, but no one believed it was a one-of-a-kind event. Meanwhile, our learned legal system debates whether restricting the sale of armor-piercing bullets—whose only known purpose is to kill human beings—would infringe upon our freedom. When cops are killers, and "cop-killer" bullets are legal, the outlook for order and justice is bleak indeed.

In the dominant culture, the poor and homeless are seen only as problems to be solved, seldom as human beings with dignity and worth. We are often surprised when someone sees them as individuals. John Fitzgerald, an advocate for the homeless, tells this story about his first meeting with Dorothy Day, co-founder of the *Catholic Worker*. He was sitting in the Catholic Worker House on St. Joseph's Street in New York City's Greenwich Village. He waited while she conversed with a drunken street woman. The woman talked loudly for what seemed an endless period of time. When they finished the conversation, Dorothy Day approached Fitzgerald and said, "Did you want to speak to one of us?" Dorothy Day was one of those people who remind us that the divine is in our midst.

Distrust of Institutions

People no longer trust institutions. We live in an industrially advanced nation where workers can be fired at will—replaceable cogs in a corporate wheel. The current economic woes (not by any means a recession, government economists are quick to inform us) have resulted in "pink slips" in many pay envelopes. Many thousands have been fired or laid off, and having this process described as "down-sizing" or "right-sizing" doesn't cushion the blow for its victims. If anything, it only emphasizes that the focus is on the corporations, not on the human beings who work for them. The corporations that decide the economic fate and personal fate of their employees tend to be governed like military states. They function without any accountability to their employees, or even to their shareholders. Corporate elites decide—behind closed doors— questions of a just wage, fair profit, plant closure, and relocation. Choices are based on profit margin and competitive marketing, not on families, futures, and years of dedication.

One area of high employment is the private security industry. Guards protect the wealthy, whether corporations or individuals, from invasion. Meanwhile, the disparity between the rich and the poor continues to grow.

Our societal malignancy is further revealed by the fact that Americans, five percent of the world population, consume fifty percent of the illicit drugs. We live in a jailed society, leading the world in the percentage of people behind bars. One-fourth of young African American men are in jail, on parole, or on probation. We've transferred the ghetto of the inner city to an institutionalized penal system.

Education in many large cities is a custodial process whose product is, ironically, illiteracy. In Toronto and Chicago I learned firsthand that some high school graduates cannot read or write, which is news to no one. Inner-city transportation is expensive, inadequate, and unsafe. Deregulation of the airline companies has led to unprecedented bankruptcies, mergers, and takeovers. Airplanes and automobiles lie on the ash heap of obsolescence in a culture whose failed gospel is insatiable greed and runaway competition. Negative economic indicators have driven people into an experience of terror and unjust strategies for survival. Once proudly known as the "motor city" for its place in the automobile industry, Detroit, like other industrial centers, is dying. The rise in murder and domestic violence is directly related to the economic insecurity that confronts this "factory town," and it is not an isolated example. The evidence that people have increasingly found themselves distrusting institutions is overwhelming.

Even the institutional church has come under suspicion. More than thirty years ago the Second Vatican Council gave birth to an understanding of church as the People of God. This vision of church generated hope, promised peace, and pointed to a place where justice could be experienced and realized. Painfully, this model of church has not survived the years since the council. For many, the church seems unwilling or unable to respond to the accelerated pace of our contemporary culture. Richard McBrien, theologian and author, suggests that many in the Catholic tradition have become "congregational Catholics," people who live their faith while disconnecting themselves from the structures of leadership that are so central to their experience of church. Others have migrated to other denominations in an attempt to find faith without dogma. We have become, as sociologist Wade Clark Roof writes, "a generation of seekers, who are more often believers than belongers."

In Latin America the ecclesiastical chasms are great. A popular church is being born out of the lived experience of people who gather in base communities to reflect on their lives in the light of the gospel. Their experience of poverty and oppression is starkly juxtaposed to the institutional church, which is often aligned to military regimes and more concerned with building cathedrals than building a people of God. These people, like many in North America, experience the church as dysfunctional.

Though many are finding their focus for justice outside the confines of the institutional church, others are creating what Paulo Freire calls "free space," a context from within the structures of their tradition where they can work to realize their vision of peace and reverence for the integrity of creation.

Whatever approach people are taking to the institutional church, however, the days of unquestioning trust in its leadership are over.

Distrust in the Political Arena

There is also evidence of a growing mistrust in the political arena. Statistics indicate that elected representatives in fact represent less than one percent of the populace. These alarming figures come home to us when we realize that half of those eligible don't vote. This step away from involvement in the political system is an echo of a deeper alienation from Earth.

Senator Bill Bradley of New Jersey says, "One pattern becomes clear. The collapse of standards. Another bank fails . . . another high school graduate can't read, another politician lies. We face a crisis of meaning. Without meaning, there is no hope."

Mario Cuomo, Governor of New York, agrees. "A million children a year are leaving school for the mean streets. . . . Some of them are growing up familiar with the sound of gunfire before they've ever heard an orchestra. Nearly a whole generation [is] surrendering in despair."[4] Cuomo challenges us to "create opportunities for all people, not just the fit and fortunate—the neediest deserve the most help from the rest of us."

We have inherited a frightening legacy from industrialization and its false promises. Seeing the world as a machine, we have learned to treat nature and other people as if they had no inherent value. This alienation from Earth and from the political process shows up in unjust systems of oppression such as sexism, racism, classism. We desperately need to leave behind all these systems of domination and control. We need to get off the ladder of domination and extend support and recognition to others—*all* others—to the entire Earth community. This journey is not an individual crusade. We need to join others and seek a new perspective so that we can take action to revitalize our culture, to create hope instead of ever-darkening despair. We need one another in order to see the divine plan written in the cosmos and act to bring about its fulfillment.

Knowing that the notion of equal political representation has been more symbolic than real enticed me to get involved in community organization. Properly developed, neighborhood organizations are able to represent at least 10 percent of the community, involving local people *directly* in the destiny of their own community. Over the years I have consistently found myself seeking sources of energy in cultural movements that promise a culture of life rather than the predictable, dominant culture of death.

Gerald Kleba talks about empowering the people in an inner-city parish in St. Louis.[5] From obtaining a needed stop sign in front of the church to organizing a parish credit union, planting a community garden, and setting up a day care center, community action became a hallmark of Kleba's "people parish." It is a book of hope. The title, of course, is a play on Scripture: "Without a vision, the people perish." Through community action, Kleba's people developed their vision.

Community action isn't reserved for inner-city parishes. We are all challenged to be cultural workers. Our task is to rediscover the sacredness of life and Earth. As we awaken to the divine presence in all of life, we will gain a new respect for the natural, new reverence for the mystery that enfolds us. We need new vision, new hope in order to confront the culture of death that surrounds us, the disappointment we feel with corporations, politics, education, and the church.

We need new symbols and ideas to fuel our imaginations because people are starved for community and rituals of celebration. Something as simple as a meaningful family meal can refresh and revitalize the spirit as well as nourish the body. In a society where 60 percent of meals are eaten alone, we have much to accomplish.

To transform the roots of war, poverty, and ecological devastation we need to develop more sensitive and sustainable ways to bring about peace and abundance on planet Earth. In an era that marks the end of communism, the end of nationalism, and an increased sensitivity to the spirit, will, and intelligence, we need to draw on ecology, theology, science, and social change. Each of these approaches will converge in the centrality of the new story of the universe we are beginning to tell.

The day of the individual prophet must be replaced by prophetic communities. In the process of liberating our culture, we are called to heal both the biocide of the planet and the genocide of people of color and ethnic difference as we celebrate our inherent connection and call to liberate Earth and its peoples. We must become aware, as Alice Walker put it, that "when we cut the tree our arm bleeds," and that no one is truly free until all are free.

The Opaque Dimension: A Watershed Moment

The pathology of contemporary culture springs, in part, from our resistance to accepting the basic dynamics of nature. When we embrace the natural order, we see that the human condition is not something separate from the natural world, but rather is intrinsically interwoven with the destiny and nature of the universe. We begin to understand, or at least appreciate, the Native American traditions with their emphasis on harmony with Earth. With this perspective we begin to see the inappropriateness of a lawn in the desert rather than cactus and sand.

Gaining this awareness is not easy. We are surrounded with messages that praise bending nature to our will. I remember looking at a popular home improvement magazine not too long ago. It presented three homes that had won awards for design and comfort. One of the three was in Arizona, and the article praised the builders for bringing a touch of their native Michigan to the desert. With massive irrigation they had managed to create a green lawn surrounded by a white picket fence. The planet can ill afford this type of self-indulgence. It would have been better if the magazine had shown the beauty of a home that existed in harmony with its surroundings. The divine is in every setting; we need to learn how to see. Earth-centered education can open us to the news from planet Earth. When we acknowledge Earth as our primary classroom, we internalize the mystery of the natural world. We see the divine in our midst. As hope springs forth in the heart of a hostage during years of incarceration, new life sprouts from dark Earth each spring.

The Voyage into Action

Today the stakes are high and the challenges great. As we survey the need for healing in our culture, we need to change both the cultural structures and our interior life. John Weir Perry, author of *The Heart of History* and a leading transpersonal psychologist, asserts that we must bring together the personal and the political. He, like David Spangler, the well-known author and educator, points out that we have enormous wisdom revealed to us by the new science and our spiritual traditions. He also understands that putting these insights into practice is very new. The disparity between the depth of insights and the capacity of translating them into action is an enormous challenge that brings a high degree of frustration. T.S. Eliot writes of this when he says, "Between the vision and the act lies the shadow."

We need to embrace that shadow. The shadow side of our personality contains chaos, but also energy. Indeed, there is great power buried in the shadow. I remember a workshop in Toronto. Gathered in groups, we were to try to see into our shadow side and then express it in some way. There was more energy in the room that day than I have ever witnessed; people were moving, singing, and creating in ways that I had never experienced before. There is transformative power when we unleash our dark side, and claim our strength.

There is so much need for change in our culture: war into peace, gender violence into justice, devastation into ecological balance, narcissism into cosmic consciousness. The opportunities that confront us are immense; the questions too big, too magnificent, too mysterious to be fully grasped. We need to confront the questions of the culture in a way that is specific and possible.

Our challenge is to live these questions with an open heart that is passionate, vulnerable, and joyful. We are confident that the questions contain within them the seeds of resolution. In our awareness we recognize the needs of the planet and its people. Robert Kennedy's words encourage us: "When we enter the moral conflict of the globe we will have allies on all parts of the planet."

One way to bring together our internal life and the world around us is to follow the insights of Dr. Jonas Salk, the prophetic doctor who developed the polio vaccine. He says that if we get close enough to nature, we will tap the wisdom within nature itself to "find the answer." Our capacity to think *like nature* will help us bridge the divisions in ourselves and become participants in a new and vital culture.

This present moment is not only an opportunity to heal the dualism between religion and science, spirituality and justice, psyche and society, but to accept that we are all totally involved with one another. The words of Dag Hammarskjöld convey well our desire to express compassion for the culture and Earth as we embark on our voyage into action: "At some moment, I did answer 'yes' to someone or something. And from that hour I was certain that existence is meaningful."[6]

For Meditation . . .

Whoever fights monsters should see to it that in the process he does not become a monster. And when you look long into an abyss, the abyss also looks into you.[7]

We have what we seek.
We don't have to rush after it.
It was there all the time,
and if we give it time
it will make itself known to us.

. . . if you want to identify me,
ask me not where I live,
or what I like to eat,
or how I comb my hair,
but ask me what I am living for,
in detail,
and ask me what I think
is keeping me from living fully
for the thing I want to live for.[8]

Questions for Reflection and Discussion

1. The news from planet Earth reveals that we are living in the "dark night of our cultural soul." How do you experience the implications of this statement?

2. To live in an anti-Trinitarian culture is to oppose the tendencies to renewal and rebirth. Explain.

3. How do you understand the words of Ralph Waldo Emerson: "They have seen but half the universe who have not been shown the house of pain"?

4. The opaque dimension and cosmic shadow name the mysterious quality of dark forces in the natural world. How do you understand this?

5. "Things as we know them are falling apart . . . people know that something is wrong . . . a whole society is coming to realize that it must drastically change its course." What is your response to this reflection from Earth Day 1970?

6. Design, script, portray, and present a "Theater of the Oppressed Earth." Engage the audience in reflecting on the questions posed during the dramatic presentation.

A Spirituality of Earth

There arises a spirituality in which the human city is human not simply by the fact that it is made up of persons and institutions; plants, the water, the pure air, the animals, and healthy conditions of natural life are also to be brought together in harmony.

Leonardo Boff[1]

The Unfolding of Our Story

"A spirituality of Earth is a homecoming. I've never felt so free, so alive, and so close to being who I really am; it has truly opened up a new way of looking at Earth and the meaning of life. My search now continues with a new lens, a lens of zeal, vision, passion, and generosity for becoming a hospice worker for a dying culture and a midwife for an ecological era that is being born." This was how one friend described her new vision.

A spirituality of Earth embraces all of our experience: the beauty and pathos of our lives, our fondest hopes, our deepest disappointments, and our most profound acts of creativity and compassion. In honoring the totality of our lives we find within apparent opposites increased wisdom and deep truth. We open ourselves to what is both ancient and new; we reflect on the origins of the universe while celebrating the most recent insights of contemporary culture. We search for meaning and purpose, and we trust that chaos itself will serve as an indicator of emerging directions in a continuing process of reflection and change.

A spirituality of Earth celebrates the mystery of the cosmos and the uniqueness of the self as diverse dimensions of the same Earth that nourishes our spirit and activates our soul. We embrace the world as a source of divine communion. We are healed of the illusion of tragic separation and alienation. Our connection with Earth honors creation, manifest in the emergence of the galaxies, the shaping of Earth, the birth of human consciousness, and our continuing development.

In our spiritual awakening we are healed of an attitude of dominance toward Earth. We see the natural world as a source of the divine. More and more we see at the heart of the universe a source of love, goodness, and affection for the entire Earth community.

We experience Earth as the source and basis of our life. We celebrate a oneness with Earth, a mysticism with the land. As we reflect on our origins, we understand ourselves and the universe as woven into an integral fabric of communion. We discover ourselves in the universe, and the universe discovers itself in us. We celebrate our journey with Earth as our spiritual journey.

We engage in a more intimate relationship with the natural world, with divine-human and interhuman relations. As we recognize and gain access to our depths, we discover the language of our souls. We discover the route of our journey in the cosmos. We reflect on the connection between death and life. We soften the threshold between the conscious and the unconscious and discern what is real and what is unreal. Earth spirituality becomes a metaphor for life that culminates in love. We discover Earth that we knew as a child. We become who we are, not who we should be. Such a spirituality has the energy to heal our hearts—and our culture.

We are entering a new era of relationships. We are learning to live and celebrate the story of the universe. Based on study, reflection, and action, we ponder the great mysteries of our time and explore our role in the emerging culture.

A spirituality of Earth is about embracing our capacity for the infinite by awakening to the beauty, pain, and consummate wisdom of Earth. Like any mystical journey, this means moving toward increasing awareness of self and body, culture and Earth.

When we look to the examples set by the great cultural workers of our time—people such as Dom Helder Camera, prophetic bishop to the poor in Recife, Brazil, Dorothy Day, and Martin Luther King, Jr.—we see that their core strength and wisdom come from their capacity to feel deeply, to love passionately, and to express outrage at injustice. They shared, as do others, a clear vision of the present and a compelling dream for the future; from this dream, and fueled by their hope, came their actions on behalf of the entire Earth community. As Martin Luther King, Jr., said, "Cowardice asks the question, 'Is it safe?' Expediency asks the question, 'Is it politic?' Vanity asks the question, 'Is it popular?' But conscience asks the question, 'Is it right?'" An Earth spirituality asks that same question: Is it right?

When I was involved in a psycho-therapeutic community in Toronto, we often spoke of "living on the threshold." We meant that place in our lives where the unconscious meets awareness. Spirituality today demands that we be willing to risk living on that threshold. We need new insights, feelings, and connection to our roots. We need to experience deeply and be fully aware of the enormous transitions taking place in our time. Our culture thirsts for this kind of spirituality. The popularity of the book and movie

Roots is a small indication of this cultural craving for connectedness. My own desire to connect with my relatives in Ireland is another example.

Awakening to the deepest reaches of our spiritual journey means becoming conscious of the sacredness of Earth and acquiring an increased reverence for all its dwellers. This awakening implicitly asks that we accept the reality that in the very depths of our being we will experience great beauty, pain, and surprise.

As we embrace new ways of seeing and experiencing our lives, we need the language of story to express and communicate our experience. In many of my classes and workshops over the years, I have discovered that story is a powerful vehicle for sharing our spiritual journey. When people share their stories of pain or mysticism, the narrative is always deep, strong, and prophetic. In the story, memory and language meet and move out to others.

Our story reveals who we are; it discloses our relationship to the entire world. Storytelling permits us to explore our inner life and learn what we truly reverence and hold sacred. Telling stories also places us in touch with our oppression. We learn what holds us back and what we fear. Storytelling speaks to us about our power and ability to act cooperatively with others.

Stories reveal the choices we have made, the obstacles we have overcome. Stories tell us who we are as a people. Some of the stories now being spoken speak clearly of pain, oppression, and injustice:

> Statistics can be cited coldly; namely of the nine hundred unarmed Palestinians shot dead since December 1987, 10 percent have been women, or again, of the eighty thousand maimed and disabled, the minority have been women. But behind each of these numbers there is a story. Narrating each story is usually a woman who is left alone to cope with conditions that are inhuman. . . . We sat under canvas and were served tea with regal dignity by women whose menfolk were either imprisoned or hospitalized. From behind their veiled costumes these Muslim women spoke with a gentle strength of resisting this oppression and pleaded with us to break the silence in the international community.[2]

These are stories we must open ourselves to if we are to join our story to those of all people and to the story of Earth.

Cultural Earthquake

Growth in fundamentalism is predictable when cultures undergo profound changes. People look outside themselves for assurances of survival, often developing an exaggerated dependence on institutions and an increased taste for rigid certitude. At the same time, others trust their inner voice rather than conform to structures and institutions that do not speak to their deeper needs.

If we opt to trust structures more than ourselves, we move toward fundamentalism. If we separate from our roots and traditions and trust only our inner experience, we risk not knowing "who our parents are," and ultimately losing our deeper selves. The challenge is to have increased trust in our inner promptings while at the same time returning to our roots. By roots, I mean that our spirituality must be based on the ancient wisdom of two books: the book of the Bible and the book of Earth. By reading the "signs of the times"— those events and aspirations that call for a response—we reinterpret our experience in light of our tradition and an evolving culture and cosmos.

Delving into the wisdom of traditions is both a challenge and a source of hope for those who have been uprooted from their ancestral homes and forced for generations into slavery in the most dehumanizing conditions. As African Americans seek foundations upon which to build in the midst of continuing oppression, stories transmitted through the ex-slave narratives, through song, and through the black church offer countless examples of wisdom, strength in adversity, courage, and hope that can inspire all who hear them:

As we read the narratives of African American slaves, a world unfolds before us. It is one that gives us a window for viewing both the oppression of slavery and the struggle for liberation. As historical and poetic documents, these stories generate plots (emplotment) and develop narratives (narrativity) for creatively communicating facts about the joys and sorrows of slaves. Consequently, along with slave folklore, spirituals, and so on, slave narratives reveal both the world they lived in as well as the one they hoped for. Moreover, they present us with the same alternative of living in the present while striving for a better future.[3]

Grandeur of Creation

The current period of profound cultural change is called a *paradigm shift*. I remember as a child going to the circus. As I watched the trapeze artists swing into the center, let go of one trapeze, and turn to meet the other, I felt consumed with anxiety. I could not bear to look. During our time of enormous cultural transition, we are like those trapeze artists. Having let go of one set of beliefs and values, we wait suspended for others to grasp.

An "ah ha" experience is an intuitive breakthrough, a radical shift in perception that culminates in and affirms our deeper knowing. To live our spiritual journey at this time of a paradigm shift is to integrate the accumulation of evidence and insight that has been building up over an extended period. We are challenged to celebrate our own "ah ha's." In effect, "ah ha" is an exuberant declaration of our own truth, that deeper knowing that is part of our lives. It unites our inner truth and the wisdom of our traditions.

Today we are reaching for a new hold, a fresh way of perceiving Earth, the culture, and ourselves. I remember in chemistry class marveling at that moment when a specific solution of the right molecular composition was combined with additional crystals to form instantaneously a collective crystal. Similarly today, the crystals of an Earth-centered consciousness are accumulating into a collective awareness of Earth. We are being reminded of the sacredness of all of life. These "crystals of Earth-centered consciousness" have unlimited potential. They might, for example, transform our schools into classrooms where Earth is our teacher, or encourage enlightened politicians to assume an ecological responsibility for the health of the people and the planet. The resulting transformation of consciousness could not help but move us forward in our journey toward healing Earth. This is our dream and our hope.

Science builds on hypotheses, but when we discover that the old hypotheses no longer explain the reality we are observing, we turn to new ways of explaining our experience. For the rebirth of our culture we must reinterpret our experience and our traditions and come to new hypotheses or paradigms. All this work takes time—decades, even generations.

To re-vision and reformulate our journey, we need to accept that nature is alive. When we do, metaphors of domination and machines melt before a unified perception of a living Earth understood as a sacred organism. We affirm that the culture and the cosmos have instinct and mind. The insights of modern physics demonstrate that there is no evidence for separation; life is holistic and interconnected. The machine is no longer a viable metaphor, and dominance is not an appropriate approach to relationships. Images of interdependence, such as the web, better reflect how we see the world.

We celebrate the capacity of the culture to organize itself, to form patterns of relationship that are conscious and alive. The conviction that Earth and culture are alive and conscious profoundly alters our attitudes and perception of everything. We have the potential to experience the sacred in a new way and acquire a fresh reverence for the living Earth.

This spiritual awakening is the only hope for arresting the ecological crisis and devastation of Earth. It forms the basis for transforming domination and devastation into reverence and interdependence. Distance and separation, in my experience, are the sources of conflict and destruction. When we become convinced of the divine presence in all things, distance and separation become meaningless. When we feel ourselves "soaked" in the divine, we realize our connection to Earth and all things. We experience unity and new life.

Our spirituality energizes us to become pilgrims rather than tourists on Earth. This is expressed innumerable times in myth, story, image, and symbol. British biologist Rupert Sheldrake reminds us that we are pilgrims when we go to a sacred place; pilgrims travel with the hope of being inspired and to express gratitude. This experience will be most meaningful when we learn the stories of the place and feel its spirit. Hiking on Inisbofin Island off Ireland's West coast with a botanist, marine biologist, and an archaeologist, seeing the region through their eyes and meeting the local people, brought this home to me. Friends who have visited Stonehenge in

England or the monasteries of Tibet have confirmed this awareness. Life, as the poster reminds us, is a journey, not a destination.

One indicator that marks the extent of our interconnectedness is the development of global communications. CNN, for example, became a vehicle both for bringing the events of the war in the Persian Gulf into our homes and for orchestrating the new Soviet alliance by bringing Mikhail Gorbachev and Boris Yeltsin into our living rooms to conduct their diplomacy. This technology can be put to the service of peace—or not. Marshall McLuhan pointed out long ago that increased communication has transformed Earth into a "global village." Seeing Gorbachev and Yeltsin, and other major political figures from distant parts of the world, speak in real time to each other can begin to heal us from the alienation of feeling that such people are forever beyond our reach. The telecommunication network we possess today can be placed in the service of creating a web of planetary interdependence.

Indeed, some steps have been taken in this direction. Electronic networks connect people all over the globe. Geonet, Green Net, and Earthnet are specifically dedicated to work for peace, justice, and ecological balance. These fiber optic strands are part of a web drawing us into closer and closer relationship.

Western psychology and medicine have begun to move from a preoccupation with pathology and to extend their focus to include healthy relationships with a healthy Earth. Unlike allopathic medicine, pain is not just a transaction in the nervous system; it is an invitation into mystery. It is shaped as well by gender, religion, class, and emotional states. Pain tests our courage and may make us stronger. It can open us to meaning. Such pain is not something to be removed like a diseased gallbladder or appendix. We need to find a place for our pain. It calls attention to the whole system, always pointing beyond itself. It can invite us into contact with the divine.

As we develop our sense of responsibility for Earth, we come to a determination to live out the commandments of creation: You shall remove all poison from the air; you shall cure all pollution of the water; you shall be open to the life-giving radiance of the sun; you shall support the self-sustaining forces of the universe. As we grow in appreciation of the natural beauty of animals, trees, and land, we can say with Gandhi, "Earth and heaven are one."

Today many people feel homeless, out of place in their bodies, in their families, and in their traditions. In many ways the homeless on our city streets dramatically project the more deep-seated homelessness in our culture. The movie *The Fisher King* portrays homeless people who have descended to the streets in the wake of a devastating trauma, a death, a war, the witnessing of a murder. It illustrates how retrieving the "holy grail" of self-respect and love helps them retrieve a balance in their lives and become liberated from the imprisonment of the street. Our search for a spirituality of Earth is an avenue for coming home to the cosmos, to Earth, to our souls, to ourselves. We need not remain homeless.

When we examine our underlying attitudes toward ourselves and our lives, we see anew how the ecological devastation of the rain forest, the extinction of whole species, the poisoned landfills, the inner cities ravaged by cocaine and racial hatred, and the crack in the ozone layer are related to the crack in the streets.

Renewed relationships to ourselves and the world can help us respond to these stirrings in the culture and understand this time of paradigm shift as an exodus moment, a movement from oppression to the dream of new life promised by God and hoped for throughout the ages.

The creation and incarnation are not over and done with. They are dynamic and always new. Our creation story is intimately connected to the creation story of the universe. When we are deeply moved by the awesome beauty of the rocks, the water, and the trees, and experience fully the colors, sound, and movement of Earth, we realize that our destiny is connected to the future of the planet.

The Cosmic Shadow

Juxtaposed with this awesome beauty lies a cosmic shadow. There is an opaque dimension to the universe, just as there is in our psyches. It is the place where pain is perpetrated and violence is expressed. To restore and heal the planet, we need to let go of the devastating practices of our cultural past. Dealing with the cosmic shadow means bringing our infinite desires into line with finite possibilities. At the center of every truth is paradox; our journey is a movement from narcissism to mysticism, from a perspective of comparison and competition to an experience of unity and beyond-ness.

One of the experiences that most evokes insecurity in people is coming to the table afraid that there will not be enough to eat. This fear can upset people, and create competition and sometimes violence. It can be resolved only when people drop their focus on their own desires and decide to live within the limits of their fair share. We need to learn this lesson and apply it in many places: in the use of water, the growing of food, the building of homes, the consumption of non-renewable resources, and much more.

Bishop Desmond Tutu, the South African opponent of apartheid, has challenged us to make sense of human suffering. The pain of our lives can be fuel for our journey. Pain can provide energy and insight. When the oppressed of Soweto Township in South Africa reflected on their pain, they found the energy and insight to name their oppression and to envision responses that transformed their pain into freedom. The African National Congress led by Nelson Mandela has begun to change political policy, including voting rights, to deconstruct the government's legitimization of racism. There is still much to be done, but there is already more hope among the people and new possibilities for justice.

Saul Alinsky, the prophet of community organization, demanded that the work of community organization require us to rub raw the sores of discontent and help people to find their pain. When the oppressed enter into their pain, they become aroused and find the energy to respond and act in new ways. Rather than being buried in depression and despair, they take action to relieve their pain and its causes. When they view their personal pain from the larger perspective of Earth, when their pain becomes cosmic, they tap the resources needed to engage in a healing process for the culture and the planet. The diverse theologies that attempt to name and transform the pain of the oppressed speak clearly of the need of those who have been without voice for so long: liberation theology, black theology, feminist theology, womanist theology, and others united in their goal of a full human life for all.

Liberation can also begin at the personal level. When friends of Richard Price, the co-founder of Esalen,[4] gathered to celebrate his life and death, they remembered his years of depression and the violence of the many insulin shock treatments that were part of his medical therapy. They also remembered how he was later liberated from that depression when he was surrounded and supported by his friends while experiencing the upset that rose from within. Suffering was the doorway to his healing. To acknowledge it, his friends chanted these lines at his wake:

And his life was full of pain
At first it drove him crazy
And then it drove him sane.

At a workshop where people sought to access and express the pain of Earth, one exercise was called the "Tree of Pain." Each participant named his or her pain by writing it on a paper "leaf" and placing it on the tree. Several clusters of pain emerged: the pain of those who had been abused, those victimized by authority, those who felt helpless at the devastation of the wilderness, those experiencing sexual oppression, those wounded by abandonment and isolation. One man, a retired minister from Winnipeg, told of a trip to Canada's Northern Alberta; he saw firsthand how the oil companies had thoroughly ravaged the forest, permitting the exposed topsoil to be blown away by the winds. A woman spoke movingly about childhood sexual abuse and how the pain has lingered into her adult life. As people shared their pain, there was a profound experience of mystery and meaning among us. Their pain loosed their tongues; it gave them back their voice enabling them to name their oppression and move forward toward liberation.

In our spiritual journey we enter the cycle of death and rebirth that is woven into the very fabric of Earth. Being willing to enter the darkness of our own psyche and embrace its opaque dimension is a necessary prerequisite for creativity and new life. As generativity emerges from emptying and death, the paschal mystery takes on a new meaning for our spiritual journey. The universe too resonates to the dynamics of life, death, and rebirth, of expansion and constriction. From the beginning of creation the cosmos has continued to unfold; simultaneously, gravity exerts its pull toward togetherness. From this dynamic tension, creativity happens.

New Era of Creativity

It is our challenge, privilege, and duty to move into a new era of creativity. Our dream is nothing less than for a rebirth of our cultural soul. Earth is a tremendous example of creativity. Babies of all species are born, seeds become plants, winter gives birth to spring, night becomes day. New life is evident everywhere. This persistent urge of creation embraces the dimensions of freedom (expansion) and containment (gravity), opening us to change and chance.

When we experience the creative process, we are always inspired. I recall participating in a liturgical ritual during a gathering north of Toronto. The Liturgy of the Word involved several groups who gathered around common interests. The music, movement, and awareness that resulted were amazing. Stories were told, songs composed and sung, drama choreographed, scripted, and presented. A woman read a poem, accompanied by a song. A man reported what it is like to be a man in an oppressive culture. A woman invited others to tell their stories of justice-making.

Earth, as a source of creativity, is a context for renewing the culture. When we die to alienation from Earth, we die to being cut off from our bodies. When we die to gender conflict, we rise to a new way of life on Earth, one that celebrates the gifts of sexuality. A spirituality of Earth is our vision for the future; it draws us forward into a compelling commitment to nurture our planet and bring joy to its peoples. We hope for a natural world and a human community integrated through new stories, structures, and ways of living.

One very practical way in which we care for Earth today is by recycling. We take our own shopping bags to the market to carry food home. We place bottles and cans in containers for use again. It seems unimpressive, perhaps, but it is a start; it is one small step toward a culture in harmony with Earth. Perhaps it helps us to see more clearly that structures and systems can also be recycled, renewed, and re-created. Patterns can be restored, structures changed.

The Interconnected Web

A spirituality of Earth channels the creative energies of Earth community into a web of interconnected energy. Leaders of the women's and men's movements are talking together in public gatherings to heal generations of misunderstanding and conflict. New dictionaries reflect our culture's new understanding of language, Earth, and the people of Earth. All across the planet, people are fashioning lifestyles that are ecologically sound and offer restoration to the planet.

A spirituality of Earth is about awareness, depth, and story. It is our hope for renewing the face of Earth and ourselves in union with it. We are able to say with William Anderson, author of *The Green Man*, that a spirituality of Earth is "the act of transforming the greening of life into the gold of the new civilization." This vision of a new civilization will tap into the reservoir of our fullest potential. We will access the forces of the cosmos, affirm our intuitive powers, and energize the impulse for compassion toward Earth.

A spirituality of Earth will empower us to transmit into the culture patterns of relationship that are folded into the dynamics of Earth. Living from this perspective, we will be able to see into the heart of things and bring into being alternative strategies for living.

A spirituality of Earth is a profound affirmation of life; through insight, experience, and expression, we celebrate, change, remember, and act into the future; we awaken to the depths and unfold our story with Earth in mind. A spirituality of Earth confronts the "death wish" of a culture that is in decline. It takes us far beyond introspection and moral imperatives. We become imbued with a reverence for life, find a place for joy and pain, and celebrate meaning rather than our accomplishments. As the current cultural dream—turned nightmare—recedes into economic recession, industrial decay, and international debt, we reach for a new sense of what is important and valuable. Earth is our vehicle for hope. In a society where political representation for all is a myth, we search for another way. In a nation where bombs take precedence over bread, and the arms race over the human race, we know something is dreadfully wrong and we look for another perspective. Our dream is to create, not to destroy.

For Meditation . . .

In 1856, in the area today called New York, the chief of the Duwamish was asked to sell the land of his ancestors. On this occasion he gave a speech that has become famous. He compared the way of living of the Indians with that of the white people. For him, the decisive difference lay in the kind of religion that the two peoples professed. Your religion, he said, was written upon stone tablets with the iron finger of an angry God so that you wouldn't forget it. This religion has always been strange to us Indians. We have never understood it and have never taken it into our hearts. Our religion is based upon the dreams of our forebears and the visions of our chiefs and the ways of our ancestors.[5]

Questions for Reflection and Discussion

1. Describe in some detail your experience of and understanding of a spirituality of Earth. What are the questions that live in you regarding this?

2. How has your experience of the cultural earthquake contributed to your interest in spirituality and altered your relationship and trust in institutions?

3. Name the moments of cultural creativity that have punctuated your spiritual journey.

4. How does our inability as a people to be at home in the universe contribute to our incapacity to find a solution to the problem of homelessness in our cities?

5. How will a healthy spirituality of Earth foster a response to the cultural and ecological crises so that the human city and natural life can be brought together in harmony?

Geo-Justice:
A Preferential Option
for Earth

I pledge allegiance to the soul of Turtle Island
  One ecosystem
  In diversity
  Under the Sun
  With joyful interdependence for all.

Gary Snyder[1]

As members of Earth community, we stand at a crossroads of momentous proportions. Sixty-five million years ago, dinosaurs, for reasons still unclear, became extinct. Their passing marked the close of an era. Today, another planetary era is coming to an end, but for reasons that are far clearer. A vast devastation is being unleashed on Earth: Species are dying, water is unfit to drink, oceans are being destroyed, soil is eroding, oil slicks and burning oil wells wreak havoc on Earth, bridges are collapsing and roads deteriorating, and more and more children are abandoned to live on the streets of our cities. Meanwhile, the primary structures of our world community—our nation-states, corporations, churches, and schools—contribute to oppression and death. This profound time of crisis and transition calls for a response, which I call geo-justice.

Geo-justice is a personal and planetary challenge to discover the converging terrain between social and environmental justice. It is a call to action that is both passionate and practical, an action that opens us not only to the crisis of our times but to the primal beauty of our Earth. Those of us living at this critical moment are challenged to liberate Earth and its peoples. We are called to practice geo-justice.

The Emergence of Geo-Justice

We are beginning to awaken from a deep cultural trance and perceive the pain of Earth and its peoples. We are approaching a watershed moment that marks the beginning of a cosmological shift in Earth's history. But with this shift comes the need for a new way of seeing and a new way of acting. The implications and proportions of this task are enormous.

Cultural indicators, such as the removal of the Berlin Wall, the formation of a new Soviet Alliance, and the 200 million people who participated in Earth Day 1990 are societal signposts of profound historical change. We also have our signs of denial in this time of transition. For example, while it is clear that the petrochemical age is coming to an end, that our dependency on oil must come to an end, we still go to war over it. We must choose the direction we want to go. The words of Scripture (Deuteronomy 30:19) have compelling relevance to the situation at the end of the twentieth century: "Today, I call heaven and Earth to witness against you: I am offering you life or death, blessing or curse. Choose life, then, so that you and your descendants may live."

This crisis demands that we discover new ways to live out our vocational destiny, new ways to become participants in a harmony, balance, and peace that Earth already knows. We need new ways of becoming instruments of an Earth-centered compassion. Just as iron filings are drawn by a magnet or as individual flames coalesce into a large fire, we are approaching a crystallization of consciousness. We are getting closer and closer to a collective awareness that supports and expands mutually enhancing relationships with Earth. Geo-justice, in a phrase, is a preferential option for Earth.

Geo-justice can be seen as the paschal mystery that locates itself within Earth. The cross is the death of the world's tropical rain forests, the struggle of starving people in Ethiopia, the tragedy of AIDS, and the erosion of our cultural soul from drug abuse. The surprise of resurrection, inexorably connected to the cross, is found in the delight in the rhythm of ocean waves, the caress of an evening breeze, the rich promise of a plowed field, the coming of spring, the touch of a loved one, the joy for a newborn child, the impulse for human rights, and efforts toward ecological balance.

In geo-justice we journey from the empty tomb of cultural collapse and a devastated Earth into a new era of novelty, surprise, and continuity marked by a new people and a new Earth. This new creation will be more about love than laws, more about harmony than competition. It will be nourished by listening to Earth and being open to the creative process emerging from within the whole Earth community.

Geo-justice is always a work of the heart, more about compassion, engagement, and participation than about reaction, obligation, and separateness. Geo-justice brings about inspiration and hope as we awaken to the sacred dimensions of the Earth community. It invites our participation in the fabric of compassion woven within Earth. In it we see our future and well-being intimately connected to the well-being of the planet.

Cosmic Crucifixion: Dying as a Transforming Act

At this time in the life of the planet, when our world of wonder, this dazzling array of life we call Earth, is fast becoming a wasteland, we are invited to be hospice workers and sit at the bedside of dying institutions. Geo-justice demands that we let go of old structures and create something new that is allied to the dynamics of bringing new life to the planet. It goes beyond the futile hope of resuscitating dying institutions. Rather, it is about putting our vital energies where there is the potential for life and not more death.

As winter follows the fall, we must face the hard death of old ways created by the petrochemical era. For example, we need to pollute less by creating an alternate means of transportation. In many ways we must become midwives engaged in the delivery rooms of cultural creativity to bring about new structures, new stories, and new forms, while we let go of the hysteria of consumption, our response to advertising and addictive behavior.

My experience confirms that illness can be a source of transformation, a doorway to new life. Human cancer is the runaway reproduction of specific cells that divert needed nourishment from other, healthy cells. In similar fashion, we suffer from a cultural cancer by the predatory draining of the world's resources away from life-giving work to producing an uncontrolled proliferation of weapons and waste.

AIDS, the erosion of the immune system, is one of the most terrifying illnesses of our time. Yet, people afflicted with AIDS are often sources of hope and life's deeper meaning. A man with AIDS captured this reality with these words: "Avoid the virus but expose yourself to AIDS." Correspondingly, Earth is afflicted with a weakened immune system brought on by pollution, pesticides, and neglect.

As we plunge into the dark night of our cultural soul, we come to terms with the grief of the planet and become open to the dazzling array of life emerging among us. From the perspective of geo-justice we see that the cosmic crucifixion can lead us into wellsprings of hope, if we bring new vision to this critical moment of collapse and devastation. Death can be the doorway to new life, an avenue toward vitally needed transformation.

Making Our Easter With Earth
If the cosmic crucifixion is going to lead us to new life and transformation, we must die to our alienation from Earth, to a dualistic

world view that separates women from men, rich from poor, people from the planet. We must die to addictive patterns of living that substitute products for people, and capital for the dignity of labor. When I met Paulo Freire, he described his work as an educator as "making my Easter." For him, to engage in education was to die and to resurrect. This archetypal metaphor for the paschal mystery is an appropriate one for the work of geo-justice, for Earth is both crucified and restored to new life. Making our Easter with Earth is also about dying to the absolute authority of our governments and public leaders, whether they are in Washington, Ottawa, London, or Tokyo. We need to listen, and rise to the radical collective wisdom emerging from reflections taking place in church basements, living rooms, and community gatherings. Dying institutions cannot lead us into the future. Rather, new visions and new forms must be generated from the narrative that unfolds when communities talk together about their relationship to the land.

Although it is about sacrifice, geo-justice is not about abstraction, obligation, and denial. It is holistic and fully connected and grounded in Earth. Geo-justice is not an anthropocentric alternative to true healing; it is an approach to liberating Earth and its peoples.

Geo-justice weaves together the global, local, and psycho-social. For example, the rubber workers in the Amazon rain forests first became concerned about the forests because their livelihood was at stake—a local concern. Gradually they joined forces with the global effort to save a resource precious to all the world. In the process they developed a deeper understanding of their own potential and power, a psycho-social dimension. Thus, each component affects and is affected by the other. Making our Easter with Earth, then, is about working with these three components as we search for language and images for our common work.

Seeing that we are one with Earth is the starting point of geo-justice. This unitive experience with the planet is necessary for global solidarity and peace. This awareness of Earth as *one* has erupted into human consciousness. In the words of Thomas Merton, we have "awakened from the dream of separateness." One of the great treasures the astronauts brought back from the moon was the image seen through the window of their spacecraft: the singular image of a blue-green, living Earth. Without this starting point of global unity or oneness, our experience on Earth will continue to be one of divisions of nations, of gender, of class, of race, of haves and have nots. When we awake from this illusion of separateness, however, we become architects of a new world order. We celebrate our oneness with Earth as we take up the challenge to think of the cosmos while acting both globally and locally.

Geo-justice is about being fully present to the sacred space we live in. It was because of where they lived that the rubber workers of the rain forests became connected to one of the primary life systems of Earth. Locally is where we tell our personal stories of Earth, where the needs of our people are heard. When we remember our relationship to the land, we make a psychic pilgrimage that connects us with the Earth as a sacred place. When we weave together a tapestry of relationships to celebrate our connection to Earth, we are propelled into prophetic action.

We come to understand Earth's oppression as our own. We see our interior life linked with the entire universe; the mystery within as great as the mystery without. Historically, justice workers have fallen into an either-or mentality. In most programs of preparation for service (ministry, social work, and so on), personal development is always seen as a precondition for action. As a community organizer, I witnessed the destruction of marriages, the fracturing of relationships, and the erosion of personal health in the name of what was best for the community. Alternatively, I have seen people go into therapy and lose sight of the importance of politics and structures as a basis for change. For some people, their outrage about injustice was more a result of their personal problems than of the systems of oppression.

Geo-justice challenges us to embrace our interior life and the world around us as one, to heal the fragmentation from within and our alienation from Earth. To connect our personal pain to the pain of the cosmos requires a single awareness. We need to access the healing properties of the psyche and deepen our compassion for Earth through vision and action that are unifying and holistic.

Emergence of a Planetary Pentecost

Pentecost is the energy of interconnectedness within the psyche and our political and social systems; it is a descent into a deeper understanding of the interrelatedness of all life. It weaves together a fabric of relationships that heals what is broken, reunites what is separated, and re-creates the face of Earth.

At the end of World War II, singer Vera Lynn made popular "When the Lights Go on Again All Over the World," an anthem of peace for our planet, a reminder of how the world becomes interrelated when "the lights go on." As a child, as I walked down the streets of my hometown in Ontario at dusk, the street lights would suddenly come on. It always amazed me, and in some way it helped me understand the meaning of Lynn's song and the meaning of Pentecost. For me, light and fire have always meant a healing from darkness, from separation, from alienation.

Planetary Pentecost is a work of the heart. It is our response to the voice that summons us to heal the pain of Earth and its peoples. We listen to this voice by being in touch with our own pain and connecting it to Earth's pain. As in deep ecology, we see no distinction between ourselves and Earth; we see that we are one. When we respond with this mind-set, fragmentation and alienation are healed.

The phrase "cosmic ache" speaks to me of the deep abiding connection we have to Earth. The ache draws us and activates in us a sacred impulse to respond. Our response contributes to a planetary Pentecost; we discover that good things are happening and we strive to make the world better. We become a new people, a new creation in a transformed Earth.

A planetary Pentecost is hopeful, prophetic, empowering, and practical; it frees us from helplessness and despair. Growing out of the story of the universe, it is a celebration of this revelatory moment. It reminds us that justice in and through Earth flows naturally out of the processes of life.

At the heart of geo-justice is the realization that we are as much Earth as the rocks, the water, and the trees. The work of geojustice—its implication for transportation, housing, corporations, schools, churches, cities, states, nations, the land, and our own lifestyles—is our work for today and our vision for tomorrow.

Where there are ruptures in creation
  we are aroused to peace

Where there is disquietude
we are invited to balance
Where there is discord
    we are attuned to resonance
In and through the pain of our wounded planet
    we are called to make our Easter with Earth
From collapse and devastation
    we discover within the risen heart of the universe
    cosmic peace
    profound harmony
    deep balance
    compassionate resonance
    Pentecost for our planet
    geo-justice with Earth.

For Meditation . . .

We join with Earth and with each other
To bring new life to the land
To restore the waters
To refresh the air.

We join with Earth and with each other
To renew the forests
To care for the plants
To protect the creatures.

We join with Earth and with each other
To celebrate the seas
To rejoice in the sunlight
To sing the song of the stars.

We join with Earth and with each other
To recreate the human community
To promote justice and peace
To remember our children.

We join with Earth and with each other
We join together as many and diverse expressions
Of one loving mystery for the healing of Earth
And the renewal of all life.[2]

Questions for Reflection and Discussion

1. Geo-justice can be understood as a paschal mystery, story, for our time. Comment.

2. Geo-justice invites us to be hospice workers for a dying culture and midwives for an era about to be born. What is your response to this perspective?

3. How do you see a connection between the crack in the ozone layer and the crack that is sold on the streets?

4. The components of geo-justice (global, local, psycho-social) are mutually enhancing and interconnecting. Describe and demonstrate this fact.

5. Geo-justice is more about being than doing. How do you understand this statement?

The Journey Into Gender

The goal of this quest is earth healing, a healed relationship between men and women, between classes and nations and between humans and the earth.

Rosemary Radford Ruether[1]

Deep within the human heart and the universe lies a profound fascination, a biological and psychological reality called gender. Our very survival depends upon this allurement and aspiration for love. But deep within our loving resides a wound, the implications of which are profound. Not only does the pain appear in broken relationships, sexism, domestic violence, and divorce, but it also lies in the seeds of ecological devastation and destruction of the biosphere. From the 1960s, women have come together to examine the impact of political and economic oppression on their lives. Today this awareness has been broadened to embrace a concern for Earth; it is called ecofeminism, a maternal response to the entire Earth community.

Today there is even more hope for our journey into and beyond gender and for the survival of Earth. Around the world there are gatherings of men who are coming together to name their pain and release the powerful and healing energies of masculinity. As they strive to heal their relationships with their fathers, connect to their deeper feelings, and celebrate their masculinity, they, like women, are striving to heal the pain that exists in relationships between men and women.

The journey into gender celebrates the experiences of women and men in their uniqueness, in their fascination for each other, and in their common citizenship on Earth.

The Fascination

Isaac Newton was fascinated by how attraction is expressed in the universe, by the meaning of gravity. The famous story of the apple dropping from the tree was told to us in our high school physics classes. Newton developed formulas to measure and reflect this attraction that is woven into the very heart of the universe. He saw that we are part of a constellation of relationships that are mysteriously held in place by an attraction that is palpable and yet numinous.

Newton saw more than an apple falling from a tree. He saw the rain coming from the clouds to quench the thirst of a receptive Earth. He saw the ocean tides enveloping Earth, the wind embracing the waters. He also saw the magnet hold in place and express attraction for the bipolar energy of another piece of iron.

If we examine our own story, we see that we also experience and express the profound attraction woven into the universe. As a child I felt a deep sense of fascination: for the St. Claire River, the night sky, the maple tree in the back yard, and my young female playmate.

I now see that gender attraction is one dimension of those attractions that permeate the universe. It is a sacred impulse. I didn't understand it as a youth, and I don't understand it now, but as the years have gone by, I have learned to appreciate and marvel at the profound dynamic of the journey into gender. It is central to our lives, permeating every chromosome; it is embedded in our genetic coding. Irish poet Patrick Kavanagh captured this reality in his poem, "The Great Hunger."

His dream changes like the cloud-swung wind
And he is not so sure now if his mother was right
When she praised the man who made the field his bride.[2]

Both in the natural world and in the human community this mysterious attraction finds itself also focused on members of the same gender. The resulting same-sex relationships can be understood as an expression of diversity in the universe. Not only do gay and lesbian relationships face the same challenges as heterosexual ones, but they also draw opposition from the dominant culture that tends to devalue uniqueness in any form. They reflect a dimension of relationship that is *not* based on the dominance of culturally determined roles, but rather on one in which people see each other as equals.

Our journey into gender tells us who we are. Our journey into gender is at the core of the generative energy whose sacred impulse invites us into life. Whether straight or gay, married, celibate, or single, the question of gender is central to our lives.

In many ways the fascination of attraction based on gender is a source of hope. It reminds us that we are more than we seem. The fascination we feel for the other reminds us that life can be more expressive, expansive, and unthwarted. Our attraction to the other lifts the spirit, elevates the quality of our life, and promises wholeness, healing, and oneness. The promise held out by our journey into gender is the promise of love, and love with its many meanings is absolutely central to our journey on Earth. I asked a 75-year-old woman, a friend of mine, about the purpose of life. Her unhesitating answer was "Love!" Love, the numinous mystery of the grandeur of the planet, is the core of the gospel, the heart of the universe, and the fire that ignites our dream for tomorrow.

While walking along the boardwalk in Spring Lake, New Jersey, near my sister's home on the shore of the Atlantic Ocean, I met an elderly man. He began talking about the restaurant he and his wife had worked in for over forty years. He talked about his son who was a doctor in Baltimore. He talked about his other son who had just taken a new job in Massachusetts. He talked about his lifelong companion, his wife. He talked about the people, the work, and the memories he loved. Our conversation was not a resume of accomplishments, but a story about attraction and love.

The journey of gender is about the journey of love. It is about the deep "gravitational pull" that draws us forward into life. Cosmologist Brian Swimme uses the word "allurement" to name this central force. It is important to acknowledge and celebrate the experience of this cosmic force in our lives.

I like to ask students to think of themselves as having a magnet near their hearts, a compass. Each of us is drawn into life by a gravitational pull; by listening to the inner voice we can connect to what draws us on. We sense what attracts us and we respond, creating the unique trajectory of our life. This is not about analyzing, measuring, and planning our lives; the impulse of this internal compass is to remind us to listen to our interior wisdom.

Honoring our deep fascinations will take us beyond the stereotypes of pursuing the "right route" as the secret to happiness. It will take us to a place where we live moment by moment in response to our inner promptings. Each instant becomes an opportunity to dance with the gravitational energy of the universe, which consistently opens in us windows of hope and aspiration. If we respond to what most deeply moves us, we will find that love is central to our existence.

When this generative energy finds sexual expression, whether homosexual or heterosexual, a new kind of bonding can take place. A sexual relationship in the context of commitment embodies the deeper dynamics of attraction; the forces are more profound and delicate. They are also in some way a deeper expression of the attractions in the universe. Relationships lived at this level of commitment embody the dynamics of Earth in a deeper way. Such a healthy relationship expresses the harmony, balance, and peace that is woven into the universe and Earth.

When the self as lover is understood as the ecological self (identified as one with Earth), the relationship becomes both the source and center of a healthy Earth. One of the mysteries being revealed to us is that the relationship between the genders is a model and source for healing our wounded Earth. The forces that are at play in the dynamics of human gender are a microcosm of the attraction operating throughout the universe and Earth.

We have much to learn from Earth about what love, allurement, fascination—gravitation—have to teach us about life. The love between women and men has historically been presented as the archetypal image of the divine's embrace. Food, drink, and eucharistic rituals have been understood as sacramental indicators of oneness of God and people. The implications of these activities, we see now, extend to all members of the Earth community.

One way to befriend Earth is to follow the journey into gender. The attraction that people experience toward one another is one dimension of the attraction that permeates the entire universe. As we resolve the conflicts of gender, we extend the harmony of gender justice to Earth itself. Mishandling this attraction of gender is destructive. It then becomes a microcosm of the ecological devastation that is perpetuated on the planet. Gender justice and geo-justice are androgynous. The entire Earth community is on a journey into gender.

The Wound

Love brings out the best and the worst in people. Despite the fascination and the impulse for oneness that is activated by our gender attraction, it is also true that our response to gender allurements is often the source of much pain, loss, and disorientation. The fact that domestic violence is the number one crime in the United States can be traced to the conflict in relationships between men and women. The fact that over half of all marriages end in divorce is a powerful indicator of the disruption caused by difficulties in relationships.

There are many ways to look at how our lives are affected by un-
resolved issues of gender. Each of us has wounds. The same impulse that drives us to heal our wounds of separation by forming
relationships is frequently the source of new wounds and further
pain.

My firsthand knowledge is of being male. Being a man in contemporary culture involves deep pain. Here are some of the ways I
understand this experience. Men are objects in the workplace of an
economic system predicated on competition and exploitation. In
North America, the life expectancy of men is about seven years less
than women. Men are nine times more likely to be in prison than
women; they are more often victims of alcohol and drugs; and they
are more often perpetrators of crime. Boys raised by the absentee
fathers of an industrial world grow up to be absentee fathers themselves. Less than one percent of men report a healthy relationship
with their fathers. Men also spend fewer than ten minutes a day of
quality time with their family. Men are for the most part driven by
compulsive work habits. They live the myth that "more is better."

An acquaintance of mine was such a work-driven, achievement-
oriented man. For many years he had not taken a vacation. Finally,
with the encouragement of his wife and family, he planned a winter holiday in the sun. After checking into his hotel, he left his family to unpack and went immediately down to the beach. When he
lay down to relax, he had a sudden and fatal heart attack. His wife
found him an hour later. This sad but true story is so common, in
one variation or another, that it is a cliche. Many men have become
victims of the economic system they have embraced.

Men tend to have few friends. Their "friends" are the husbands
of their wives' friends. Although they may work with male associates, they largely live isolated and production-oriented lives.
They are driven to succeed but rarely experience what can be called
authentic success. The desire for monetary rewards and the drive to
dominate make the workplace a place where the wound is deepened rather than healed.

The common terms and phrases "opposite sex," "battle of the
sexes," "gender bias," and so on, reveal the antagonism between
men and women. Deep in the male psyche there is often a fear of
women. This fear is expressed in distance and sometimes in dom-

ination. It seems that men, and women too, don't know what to do with their natural attraction for each other. They barter it; they use it as a weapon or vehicle for control, or as an avenue for destruction and even violence.

It has been well documented that political and economic systems have been governed by the rule of men. This system, patriarchy, has been understood to be the unjust domination of one group by the other. Historically, this institutionalized gender-based oppression has benefited men. There is much documentation in churches, corporations, and public life of how women's opportunities are limited in regard to income, participation, and influence. The ways in which these injustices have been rationalized theologically have only contributed to the injustice.

Women have come together, motivated by the political, economic, and religious oppression they have experienced as a result of their gender. But there is still a long way to go. The ways we have oppressed Earth, forced production by injecting fertilizers into the land and steroids into animals, is a reflection of how women have been oppressed. They have been forced to produce children and submit to care-taking roles. From their wedding day, women have been counseled to be "subject to their husbands." This language has perpetuated the subjugation of women. Today we are experiencing an emergence of the divine feminine, which, accompanied by the emergence of the "green man," has created a new rationale for gender-justice.

People are in pain and facing untimely deaths because of sexually transmitted diseases. AIDS has cast a shadow over sexual contact. Young people respond to the "stirring of their hormones" by plunging into relationships that in some ways seem to be orchestrated by forces that are distant from them, or at least outside their control. Teenage pregnancies and abortions only compound the confusion. The chaos, oppression, and doubt that are propagated by an unintegrated sexuality have become metaphors for the ecological devastation that runs rampant.

No journey into gender can overlook the fact that the dominant culture has placed women in an inferior position. Our culture has posited maleness as normative and femaleness as secondary. Our journey into cultural rebirth must instead be a journey of equals, one that questions all structures of inequality and celebrates the rights, capacities, and privileges of women, men, and all creatures of Earth. The conversion from oppression to liberation will promote a healing of the brokenness and injustice that distort female-male relationships. In the past we have been blinded to the goodness of gender and the destructiveness that has characterized the allure of power and privilege. Awakening to the injustice of sexism has brought women to experience liberating outrage at the inequities of gender and a renewed sense of their own worth. Men, in turn, are just beginning to recognize their own victimization and reclaim the repressed dimensions of their multi-faceted personalities. We are beginning to understand that the vision of the future must be a shared vision, one that promises liberation for all.

The same structures that underlie the domination of women also oppress Earth. As we mismanage human reproduction, we proportionately destroy Earth by production and overproduction. We fail to care for what Earth provides: rain forests, wheat crops, cattle.

As conflict and violence surface between men and women to find expression in domestic conflict, custody battles, and competition, so war proliferates on the planet. War among nations, rage against Earth, and oppression against the vulnerability and fertility of the endangered planet result. We cannot postpone approaching our gender issue if we are going to care for our endangered planet.

The attraction between the genders holds out one of life's greatest promises: that of fulfillment and love. This promise is consistently extended to us by the gravitational embrace of the universe, a phenomenon Thomas Berry calls the "curve of compassion." Berry is referring to Einstein's idea of the "curvature of space," which holds the universe together in a delicate yet infinitely precise embrace.

When the deep desire for oneness with another person is acted upon, it is often accompanied by an unleashing of destructive forces. This paradox can become a lens through which to examine much of the destruction perpetrated on the planet.

Together men and women are discovering that gender is a verb; it is what we do. It resides more in our imaginations than in our biology. The problem is not with gender per se, but rather with the cultural forms that oppress the spirit. When experience is honored, relationships built, and empowerment fostered, we will create a future that sets both men and women free.

Chaos and the Capacity to Heal

More than two decades ago in a public forum held in New York, Norman Mailer and Germaine Greer engaged in a dialogue on gender. The event did not go well. It is reported that a lesbian couple took the stage, without invitation, and expressed a sign of affection to protest their experience of alienation and oppression. Held at the beginning of the women's movement, this event was an indication of the so-called battle of the sexes.

A similar event was held in early November 1991 in the Great Hall of New York City's Cooper Union shortly before the 25th anniversary of the founding of the National Organization for Women. It sold out within a day of being announced. Robert Bly, author of *Iron John* and poet of the new men's gatherings, and Deborah Tannen, author of *You Just Don't Understand*, were the featured guests. They had read each other's material and engaged in a conversation designed to increase understanding and listening rather than to promote slogans and division. This event was a watershed moment in the journey into gender that will guide us into the new millennium. I see men and women engaging in a process to understand both themselves and the other.

The phenomenon of men's gatherings is recent in our time. Men are searching for ways to heal the wounds that have been caused by their boyhood and the stereotypes of a sexualized culture. These gatherings are often trivialized by the media much as the women's movement was made fun of three decades ago. In their gatherings, the men strive to express themselves more fully. They read the works of Sam Keen, author of *Fire in the Belly*, Robert Bly, and many others. They strive to heal their relationships with their fathers. They attempt to overcome the alienation of three or four generations of living in an industrialized world. They celebrate their relationships with their grandfathers and the cellular relationships they have had with mentors.

In workshops and classes I have heard men talk appreciatively about their baseball coaches, their pastors, teachers, uncles, and friends. They remember how these men provided support, guidance, and understanding for them in their developing years. Men talk about their feelings and their difficulties in being able to identify how they feel. They face their vulnerability in a world where they are expected to be more like machines than men. As they examine themselves as political and economic benefactors of an unjust system, they are willing to let go of their position of dominance, while seeing that they themselves are victims. Putting aside the stereotypes of "macho" or "wimp," they come to see that it is possible to express themselves fully as strong males while *not* continuing to perpetuate injustice; that it is possible to be both feminist and pro-man. As participants in the mytho-poetic approach to men's liberation, they rejoice in the fact that it is possible to access the energy of the deep masculine and at the same time be agents of gender justice in a culture that sets both men and women free.

A promising sign of cultural rebirth in terms of gender justice is the flowering of white ribbons on American college campuses. Worn by men, the ribbons represent opposition to sexual harassment and assault. These symbols originally appeared in 1989 at a university in Montreal, Canada, where fourteen women were slain by a man who then committed suicide. Women have been saying for some time that harassment and assault are unacceptable. The ribbons send a message from men to other men that violence against women is not tolerable.[3]

As men and women reflect upon their role in society, they may come to understand that unjust oppression is not just gender based. At the heart of our culture's pathology is industrial dominance, which names our alienation from work, gender, body, and Earth.

The Green Man by William Anderson demonstrates that when there is an emergence of the goddess in the culture, there is also an emergence of the "green man," a complementary male archetype that reflects a closeness to and harmony with Earth. From the green man and goddess (the emerging divine feminine) we will fashion the gold of a new civilization of gender justice.

The gender journey is in many ways more central to our lives now than it has been at any other time in the recent past. Men are beginning to redefine themselves. There is a growing distinction in our culture between the brokenness of patriarchy and the wholeness of authentic masculinity. Feminist and Jungian psychologist

Marion Woodman has affirmed this in her writings, which have shifted the gender conversation from blame to analysis. The classical Jungian distinction of animus and anima has come to the end of its time in assisting us to understand male and female. No longer is it appropriate for a man or a woman to say, "I'm in touch with my animus" when referring to the more assertive side of the personality. Alternately, it is inappropriate to use "anima" to designate receptivity as a feminine characteristic. There are assertive and receptive qualities to both male and female aspects of our psyche. It is both biased and inaccurate to appropriate these characteristics to gender.

Men and women are discovering that roles do not define who they are; they are discovering an androgynous middle ground where consensus is possible and conflict dissolved with a new understanding of the spectrum of expressions for men and women. The animus and anima have given way to a new understanding of how men and women express themselves. No longer can it be the practice to designate destructive behavior to one gender and harmonious activity to the other.

Blame is being replaced by a gender partnership in both naming and healing the unjust oppression that is embedded in our social structures. Men who have focused on finding their fathers are now seeing the need to do work around the mother.

The vision of gender justice will be realized when women and men in wholeness merge their energies as friends and respect each other and Earth, enjoying equal compensation for their labor. They will celebrate their differences in a world where daughters won't have to be angry and sons won't have to hide their tears. Together, women and men will fashion out of their courage a "chain of hope" that will embrace and heal the forces of domination and violence in our culture.

It is becoming increasingly clear that as men and women heal the gender-based conflicts of their lives, they are also moving toward a resolution of the polarized conflict that lies at the center of cultural pathology and ecological devastation.

Something new is happening today. Men and women are responding to their hearts and to a call for life. Through music, dance, drumming, and other symbols they are responding to the pulse of the universe and the passion of transformation. Men and women as never before are seeing their individual journeys as a common journey—a cultural event that is heroic, adventurous, and that transcends differences. This window into gender harmony serves as a metaphor for planetary peace. It energizes our journey toward cultural rebirth.

Men and women are digging deeply into the recesses of their psyches. They are finding there a new source of strength that is both strong and gentle, full and empty, expressive and receptive, dynamic and liberating, compassionate and stubborn, prophetic and peaceful. Feminism, men's liberation, and gender work will be our teachers as we move into the future.

We need to foster the creative tension between men and women. As the strings are drawn over the frets of a guitar, the strings must be neither too slack nor too tight or they will be unable to provide a proper note; this is also true of the attraction that exists between men and women. Out of this creative tension a harmonious chord can be struck.

The journey into gender is about the celebration of sacredness. It involves acknowledgment, equality, and hope. For women, it means full participation in the workplace, in the practical and economic arenas. For men, it is about reclaiming the body and also healing from being treated as objects of production in a society of capitalism and competition. As women and men, our journey is not about blame and blindness; rather, it is about celebration and support. Our collective call is to move into gender—and beyond—to become new people on a new Earth, to reinvent our species, to make possible a future based on harmony and peace. Each person—man and woman—must give his or her unique gift to humanity's vision of a new culture and a new Earth.

For Meditation . . .
Whatever befalls Earth
Befalls the sons and daughters of Earth
We did not weave the web of life

We are merely a strand in it
Whatever we do to the web
We do to ourselves.[4]

Questions for Reflection and Discussion

1. What do you understand to be the connection between our relationship to Earth and the gender dynamic between men and women?

2. Reflect on your journey into gender from the perspective of fascination, wound, and healing.

3. As a woman or man, what do you understand to be the primary needs of your gender?

4. How do you see gender justice contributing to harmony between Earth and its people?

5. The journey into gender is in fact a journey beyond gender to become the new human. What are the characteristics of the new human?

Acting Globally and Locally

Creation is the first act of liberation.

Gustavo Gutierrez[1]

At this time in history we need to heal the cultural pathology by approaching it differently. We need to see it from the perspective of Earth and from a view that sees Earth as sacred. The collapse of positive economic indicators reminds us that something deeper is going on. We are experiencing a cultural recession as well as a downturn in dollars. In a time marked by a shift toward increased human interdependence and global consciousness, we also realize that neither global nor local institutions nourish and foster full participation in this new era of human and ecological relationship.

Teilhard de Chardin wrote that "the age of nations has passed. Now, unless we wish to perish we must shake off our old prejudice and build Earth."[2] With him we realize in a new way that nations are too small to solve global problems and too large to respond adequately to local problems. The world needs new structures that will provide full participation. In our concern for each person and our concern for all, we acknowledge the tragedy of events such as the violence against the students in China's Tiananmen Square or against Rodney King in Los Angeles, and we rejoice in the political epiphany of taking down the Berlin Wall. Together, we live with the question of what is yet to come.

The work of birthing a new culture is a vehicle for unleashing the relentless and unbidden impulse to embrace and give birth to the sacred aspects of life. As we become increasingly conscious of the divine in our midst, we feel the aggression toward Earth dissolve and we embrace the manifestation of beauty that envelops us. Through an enhanced awareness of the sacred mystery of Earth, we can respond with increased energy and spontaneity to the emergence of a culture attuned to the natural world.

We hope to move into a new type of culture, one where the divine becomes palpable and present. We hope to celebrate beauty, to understand attention to pain, and to ignite a new awareness of the sacred. We hope to translate the pathology of collapse and devastation into an increased capacity to love deeply, feel passionately, and express outrage at injustice. As Teilhard puts it,

> The day will come when after harnessing space
> the wind
> the tides

and gravitation
We will harness for God the energies of love

And on that day for the second time in the history of the world
We shall have discovered fire.[3]

The story of the universe and our own Earth is awesome and mysterious. It contains all our individual and cultural stories. This new cosmic story reveals the basic pattern of the universe through the principles of communion, differentiation, and interiority. When we understand how that new story or myth is connected to our own story, we tap into enormous energy and release the power for cultural transformation.

The formation of the Soviet Commonwealth of Independent States out of the ashes of the former Soviet Union is a political example of cultural transformation. The Commonwealth uses the principle of communion by drawing on the common history of the member states. This is expressed by a common flag and insignia and nurtured by remembering and recounting a history that predates the Marxist-Leninist revolution. Unlike the totalitarian Soviet Union, the member states of the Commonwealth are also striving to express their unique histories. The Ukraine, Russia, and each of the others has a different story and understanding of its past. Russian artist Julia Kirillova portrayed this reality by creating a sculpture for each of the states of the former Soviet Union. It was her way of expressing the wish of her people for a political reform and a deepening of the democratic process. The formation of the Commonwealth also demonstrated a spontaneous self-organizing aspect. When Mikhail Gorbachev initiated *glasnost* and *perestroika*, he did not foresee their far-reaching effects. Certainly he did not know that in seven years he would find his position dissolved. The process he initiated had a life of its own. Granted there will be difficulties and struggle with this new political configuration, but I believe that this new structure is more aligned to the dynamics of the universe than the previous U.S.S.R. There is communion; each member state belongs to the Commonwealth. There is also differentiation; each state is unique and diverse.

Science teaches us that in every process or reaction there is an energy loss. This loss of energy is known as entropy. Most human systems become exhausted over time. They lose energy, wear down, and finally die. Energy loss also affects social structure. After five to eight years most organizations tend to oppose the very purpose for which they were begun. They only function at the peak of their capacity for three to four years. Surprisingly, the systems of Earth suffer very little entropy. Instead of being lost, much of Earth's energy is recycled. Leaves become compost, which gives new life to new trees. Water evaporates, forms clouds, and returns to Earth as rain. By imitating the dynamics of the universe in our cultural forms, we can extend their vitality and effectiveness.

The Soviet Union, to return to my example, had no room for diversity and spontaneity. Its sense of communion was enforced totalitarianism, not interconnectedness. It eventually ground to a halt. The new Commonwealth, although having many problems, contains a greater potential to sustain itself because it is more closely allied in its purpose to the dynamics of the universe. In this way entropy is reduced and its life expectancy is extended.

We need to create rituals that express these dynamics. We need rituals as instruments of cultural rebirth. The sad fact, though, is that we live in a "ritual poor" society.

An Agenda for the New Era

Cultural transformation requires new vision, new language, new energy, and new action. We need to reconnect with the wonder and power of Earth. With increased confidence we come forward to affirm our focus and offer our gifts, strengthened by a willingness to do our inner work as we participate in the birthing of a culture of creativity and life. We listen to the heartbeat of hope as we engage the forces of oppression in our dying culture. We are stirred by the aspirations for newness that arise from the recesses of our souls. We catch a vision that both challenges us and fills us with hope. It is a vision and a purpose first glimpsed long, long ago by our forebears:

> Take the night that Yahweh called them out of their tent in the desert and asked them to look into the sky at the stars. Abram, and most probably Sarai too, must have been amazed

that they were asked to do so. They had left Ur and Haran because they felt that they should not stare at the moon and the stars any more (Judith 5:3-9). Now Yahweh asked them to do so, and they did. Looking in the bright star-studded sky they saw for the first time something in between those stars that became the leading vision all through Judaic and Christian literature. As the letter to the Hebrews so much later will recount, they didn't see it clearly yet. They only had an inkling. They saw "from a distance" (Hebrews 11:13) and from afar "the city, with foundations, whose architect and builder is God" (Hebrews 11:10). This image is fully worked out in the last book of the Bible, the book of Revelation. John describes the end, when there will be one city. God will dwell in that city, and Jesus Christ, the Lamb, will be enthroned in it. All nations will come together to the city, each one bringing its own glory and honor (Revelation 21:24-27). It is the final outcome of God's love project for the human family. It is our destiny, and our mission.[4]

We know where we are going! With Earth in mind, we participate in the incarnational event of personal and planetary rebirth.

In the loss of a loved one or the extinction of a species we connect to the pain of Earth and its creatures. Emptied through grief, we reach for transcendence. We stretch toward the vision of a new culture that puts people before the Pentagon, being before doing, peace before production, diversity before sameness, innovation before duplication, engagement before procrastination, justice before domination, and communion before fragmentation. We discover these new avenues of activity from within the processes and order of the universe itself. Our work will liberate us from the pathos and paralysis of our time. Healed from addiction and alienation, we come home to ourselves and Earth as the source of balance, newness, and peace. And we look at the stars!

To move toward our vision requires us to stop the destruction and oppression existing in our lives and cultures. We must contemplate our own origins and stories to deepen our sense of the sacred and give new meaning to the mystery and purpose in our lives.

Further, we need to find intimacy with the natural world. Doing so helps us discover our place and path within the spiritual processes of the universe itself. We see ourselves as creative participants in God's great cosmic work. We accept the challenge to be more alive to the natural world and more engaged in the radical renewal of our culture. As we connect our story and the culture's story with the ever-unfolding story of the whole creation, we discover new possibilities for personal and social transformation.

As we pursue harmony, balance, and peace, we take up our personal challenge to liberate Earth, which is much abused in contemporary culture. We make connections with others and choose together the ways to express our option for Earth. As we continue our mysterious journey in the universe, we discover new energy that enables us to respond to the urgency of our time through actions that are immediate, focused on needed changes, and based on the concrete experience of a people and a culture in crisis. Our vision of the new Earth and new culture is enlightened by ecological awareness, social involvement, and solidarity with the natural world.

Drawing on the wisdom of liberation theology, we will focus on the concrete experience of local people and engage in action to change the social and political spheres from the perspective of the poor. Liberation theology places its emphasis on action to transform the world; it is not a "head trip," but a "foot trip." Out of this we come to our knowledge of the divine. For liberation theology, reflection begins "at sundown," *after* the action. The themes of liberation find their scriptural sources in Exodus and the writings of the prophets, who denounce injustice, bringing critical awareness to the need for social liberation, solidarity with the poor, the radical restructuring of systems of oppression, and the creation of lifestyles that are coherent with our vision of a new society.

Our work should also draw on the insights of contextual theology as fashioned by Albert Nolan, who works in the anti-apartheid movement through the Institute for Contextual Theology in South Africa. Contextual theology always begins with a particular context; it starts with life, with everyday experience. Through reflection, the experiences become more conscious. When the reflections are conducted in common, they achieve directions and conclusions that cannot be achieved working alone. Through collective dialogue, we question both the group and ourselves. We do not rely on the past for answers. Current experience and questions become our starting point. Contextual theology's approach is always concrete and practical. It helps us begin and end with practice rather than with abstractions.

The cooperative movement and community organization provide a fully democratic context that flows out of our vision of equality, dignity, trust, curiosity, and work as the great task of creation. Based on the principle that the first act of doing justice is organization, we see the need and the means to confront the insatiable "more is better" approach of the dominant culture; integrated with these other approaches, the cooperative movement contributes to our vision, one that acknowledges both the limits and the possibilities of the human-Earth community.

One view of our hoped-for future is nourished by the wisdom of the new cosmology and Earth literacy being developed by Thomas Berry at the Riverdale Center for Religious Research in New York. Guided by a vision of a time of creativity for both the human and Earth communities, Berry looks toward an era when a new realization of the sacredness of life will be fostered, accepted, and protected by humankind. He posits these assumptions about Earth community:

- The universe is a communion of subjects, not a collection of objects.
- Earth exists and can survive only in its integral functioning.
- Earth is a one-time endowment.
- Earth is primary, and humans are derivative.
- There is a single Earth community.
- Humans can understand fully and respond effectively to their role in this new era.

As we reconnect with the wonder and power engendered by our intimate relationship with Earth, we gain confidence, affirm our focus, and offer our gifts. Strengthened by a willingness to do our inner work, we participate in the promptings that contribute to a culture of creativity. We listen to the heartbeat of hope emerging from our dying culture whenever we engage the forces of oppression. We are stirred by the aspirations for newness that arise from the recesses of our souls. As the possibilities well up in our hearts, we catch again a glimpse of that vision that activates our energies toward personal and social transformation, that vision that set Abraham and Sarah on their travels. We live fully and effectively, fueled by the insights of the various movements of liberation. We tell our story and create our future. As our energies converge with the prophets of our time, we gather with colleagues to address the question, What is next in our lives? We know today, as perhaps never before, that we can do together what we can never do alone. In our quest for community we "grow" our hearts—to make them bigger, more open to beauty, and more courageous in pain. As we gather to give our gift in extraordinary ways, we celebrate diversity, honor everyone's voice, and appreciate our interconnectedness. As we share our visions, we see ourselves as unique paragraphs in the great cosmic story.

Fashioning the rebirth of culture involves a narrative approach; it begins with storytelling. As our stories generate themes, we discover the commonality of our experience, which will move us into action. We connect our vision and our actions through art, ritual, and story. As we color in the stories of our lives, we reflect on moments of grace. We participate in the incarnational event of personal and planetary rebirth. We connect to the pain of Earth and its peoples when we experience death, the loss of a loved one, or the extinction of a species. Emptied through grief, we reach for transcendence. Healed from addiction and alienation, we come home to ourselves and Earth as the source of balance and peace. We discover our destiny and remember that every member of the Earth community has a sacred purpose and place.

As we have seen, the principles of the universe—differentiation, interiority, and communion—reflect the dynamics of the Trinity (Creator, Word, and Spirit). In a very real way we can say that when the principles are present, the Trinity is also present, and the divine is born among us.

As we listen to the voices of our wounded Earth, we must reverse the tendency of the dominant culture; our challenge is to celebrate community where it does not yet exist, to reverence diversity where it is denied, and to honor spontaneity where it is repressed. As we reach out in hope for a cultural rebirth, our goals include:

- conserving pure air, water, and fruitful soil
- re-visioning our view of community to include all living and non-living beings
- discovering a new language to give expression to our work and tell our stories
- exploring natural energy sources (solar and hydroelectric), while acknowledging the decline of the petrochemical era
- living closer to the land by growing food, celebrating the seasons, and exploring the sacred dimension of all nature
- developing cultural forms that are better attuned to the natural dynamics of Earth and the life of the Trinity
- restoring ecological balance and restructure political and economic relationships on a global level
- expanding our awareness of a liberating God who is on the side of the victim, the voiceless, and poor Earth
- opening ourselves to spontaneity
- reflecting upon our efforts to move into a new way of living.

Through striving to achieve these goals, we will become a sacrament for the new era that awaits us. We will bring about what we propose: a theology of newness, an harmonious relationship to Earth.

For Meditation . . .

> My heart is moved by all
> > I cannot change
> So much is being destroyed.
>
> I have cast my lot
> > With those who age after age
> Perversely,
> And with no extraordinary power
> > Reconstitute the world.[5]

Questions for Reflection and Discussion

1. Years ago René Dubois coined the phrase "Think globally, act locally." The title of this chapter has a different focus. What is your preferred perspective and why?

2. How can we learn from Earth regarding entropy and its relationship to social organization?

3. Thomas Berry writes in the foreword: "The cultural vessels of all the peoples of Earth, however diverse, were shaped and fired in [the] same primordial furnace." How will acting globally and locally contribute to this vision?

4. "The age of nations has passed. Now, unless we wish to perish we must shake off our old prejudice and build Earth." What is your response to the words of Teilhard de Chardin?

5. Consider your destiny in light of your cultural work. Why do you do your cultural work? How do you do your cultural work as your unique contribution to human-Earth relations? In what way do story, art, and ritual bring into congruence your particular practice and vision of Earth as one?

Commencement

Here on the pulse of this new day
You may have the grace to look up and out
And into your sister's eyes,
And into your brother's face,
Your country,
And say simply
Very simply
With hope—
Good morning.

Maya Angelou[1]

Creation is the first act of liberation.
Liberation's first act is organization.
Organization's first act is storytelling.
The story of creation is . . . organizing for the liberation of Earth.

To bring about cultural rebirth we need to generate many responses: a vision of hope that mediates wisdom and contacts mystery; a tangible manifestation of community and diversity that fosters inspiration and meaning; a place of purpose that responds to Earth and its peoples who suffer, who are poor or lonely, who are victims of political, economic, and social oppression.

As our culture is reborn, there must be information and support for those who work to bring about inspiration and a global dream for the future. Creating such a context of communication and truth will mean moving from systems of oppression and hurt to a place of healing, liberation, and hope. The rebirth of culture will offer the possibility of a common action where we can transform our struggle and fragmentation into a tapestry of common consciousness and hope.

As cultural workers who are energized by the quest for communication with sacred Earth and by an urgent impulse for social and ecological justice, we need to reach out to others so that together we may have whatever is necessary to generate hope, to share the vision, and to be healed where we hurt.

We have been reflecting on the world and our role in it from new perspectives. Incorporating this new view of the story of the universe into our reality takes time and mental effort. But our new insights need to move us into action. What do we do next? The liturgy concludes with the instruction to go out from the assembly and live the meaning of the community gathered in the name of the divine. We, too, need to put aside our reading and apply to our daily life what we have learned.

The following "Project Earth: A Process for Praxis" and reflection exercises will help the reader determine the direction his or her life in—and for—the cosmos will take. Some of the reflections are suitable for individuals; others should be conducted in a group of like-minded individuals, perhaps as part of a series of workshops on cultural rebirth.

Project Earth: A Process for Praxis

The Spiritual Narrative

1. Explore your internalized experience by reflecting on your story from a *personal, cultural,* and *cosmic* perspective.

2. Generate the themes that emerge from naming your experience as you reflect on:

- beauty, hope, and rebirth
- oppression, inertia, and numbed feelings
- a threshold experience: an expression of creativity and uniqueness that affected your life
- the web of interconnectedness you experience with all creation through communion and compassion.

An Action Autobiography for Earth

Strive for congruence between your world view and your concrete actions by reflecting on the following questions:

- Do you recall the first action you engaged in for the sake of change and transformation?

   What was it?

   Did it enhance your ability for future actions?

   Did you feel any sense of solidarity with others as a result of this action?

- Why do you do your cultural work? What is your motivation?

   Who are the people in your life who bring you hope, promote freedom, and give you courage and compassion?

   What are the forces of oppression, the symbols and sources of limitations in your life?

   What has been your most prophetic effort on behalf of Earth?

- How do you do your cultural work?

   In what ways have you worked toward unity between your ideas of cultural rebirth and your actions?

   How does your activity contribute to the enhancement of human-Earth relations?

   What have you learned about yourself through your actions on behalf of Earth? What have you learned about Earth?

- In what ways could story, ritual, and art mediate between your vision of Earth and universe and your particular practice?

Describe through a picture, drama, ritual, or story what has or continues to hold you back.

- How have the people in your past, and back several generations, struggled with their values and their relationship to Earth?
- How have your activities in behalf of Earth deepened your experience of the divine in concrete and tangible ways?
- What do you plan to do next? What is the next phase of your journey?

Cultural Action for Earth: The Rebirth of Culture

Ritual, art, and story shift our framework of understanding from parts to interconnectedness, from linearity to unfolding, and from conformity to creativity. They bring together action and vision. As you consider a specific activity, reflect as well on your experience of ritual, art, and story. Then respond to the following questions:

- What do you see?
- What do you feel?
- What have you done?
- What do you still need to know?
- What do you still need to do?
- How does this particular action invite you into further expressions of ritual, art, and story, leading to further reflection and renewed action?

Fashioning the Rebirth of Culture

1. Continue to provide information, support, and the possibility of common action for people engaged in the rebirth of culture.

2. Fashion the building of community as a context for diversity, listening, and interconnectedness.

3. Research the liberation movements (liberation theology, Earth literacy, contextual theology, popular education, cooperative movement) and continue through ritual, art, and story to integrate them into an action strategy to enhance human-Earth relations.

4. Be open in theory and practice to bringing peace, harmony, and balance to Earth and its peoples (geo-justice).

Reflection Exercises

Images and Gifts (Group)

Preparation: Each participant is asked to bring two items: 1) an object that is in some way an image or symbol of herself or himself; and 2) a gift to share with others in the group.

1. Ask the participants to place their gift for the others on a central altar. While they move around the altar, they may play drums and other instruments. After all the gifts have been placed on the altar, continue the drumming for several minutes while the group moves around the altar.

2. Invite each participant to show the object that represents him or her and comment on its meaning; the drumming and procession continue.

3. Ask one of the participants to select a gift from the altar. The donor steps forward and presents it, explaining why it is a gift and what meaning it has had.

4. The donor then selects a gift, and the process continues until all have chosen.

5. Form a circle and celebrate why each person has chosen his or her gift. Close with a suitable song or music tape.

Cultural Profile (Individual)

1. Identify a cultural belief or myth transferred to you by your family or culture.

2. What rituals celebrate the myth you have identified?

3. Who are heroes in your life?

4. What do you feel most passionate about when you think of Earth and humanity's place in the story of the universe?

5. If you have been doing cultural work, reflect on the reasons you have done so, what the results have been, and what you have learned. If you are just becoming involved in work for cultural rebirth, think about concrete actions you can take.

Cultural Rebirth (Individual)

1. How do you feel about "reinventing the culture"?

2. What questions do you have about working for cultural rebirth?

3. How do you understand your role as a "cultural worker" at this time?

Allurements and Letting Go (Group)

1. Invite the participants to break into small groups. To rid themselves of preoccupations, invite each person to speak for five minutes about anything on his or her mind.

2. After each person has spoken, ask the participants to empty their minds, let go, and focus on what most fascinates them.

3. After this, give the participants an opportunity to respond, individually or in groups, to any images and aspirations that arose.

4. Conclude by asking the participants to move around the room and extend a *silent* greeting to one another.

Reinventing the Human (Group or Individual)

1. Discuss or meditate upon this statement: Myths are instruments for bringing about cultural renewal; they are the mediating narratives that bring us into accord with the universe.

2. Discuss or meditate upon this statement: The story is a symbolic vehicle for affirming our basic truth; it challenges us to deepen our self-understanding and contributes to our participation in the destiny of the planet.

3. Reflect on the following in the context of the last four generations:

- What are your major concerns?
- What are your primary sources of satisfaction?
- How do you understand your position in society: its privileges, limitations, responsibilities?
- What is your image of the divine?
- What are the roots of your personal myth?
- How do you carry out family patterns?[2]

4. Reflect on the unfolding of the cosmic story. What part do you play?

Epilogue for an Era That Awaits Us (Group)
Play music softly throughout this process.

1. Invite the participants to prepare an epilogue for their lives, a kind of eulogy that names their struggle, points to what they have accomplished, and indicates what they have left behind.

2. Ask the participants to select partners with whom they exchange their "eulogies."

3. After reading the eulogies, invite the participants to circle around an altar-like table, upon which is a mattress. A chair is placed at one end.

4. As they mill about, circling the table, invite a volunteer to sit on the chair when they feel ready to participate.

5. One member of the group (the partner) accompanies the participant to the table where she (he) is covered with a blanket.

6. The person's partner reads the eulogies; the other participants place their hands on the eulogized person.

7. Finally, a drum is struck or the leader claps his or her hands. Everyone helps the person rise. Then the person is greeted by all the other participants.

8. Continue the process until each member has been "eulogized."

9. Gather in a group to discuss the exercise. Be sure each person is given a chance to talk about the experience.

Cultural Beliefs (Individual)

1. Identify a cultural belief from a myth or set of beliefs transferred to you by your family or culture.

2. Have you ever had a basic belief contradicted or confronted by a different belief? How did you feel? What did you do about it?

3. Have you ever discarded a belief because it no longer was true for you? How did you feel?

4. What was your first political experience? What did you learn from it?

5. How are heros created in your culture? Do educational institutions reinforce these heroes?

6. What cultural rituals celebrate the myths of your community?

7. What actions on your part could bring about a change of heart and mind?

Moving to Cultural Action (Individual or Group)

1. Describe how your basic beliefs about your country influence your interpretation of international events or happenings.

2. What is your source of information regarding these events? Does your source contradict or reinforce your basic beliefs?

3. What do you understand by a rebirth of culture?

4. What might bring about this rebirth?

A Project for Cultural Rebirth (Group)

1. Form groups of three to five people.

2. Ask each group to compose a manifesto or vision statement of what the group believes about cultural rebirth.

3. Ask each group to prepare an action strategy to implement its vision statement.

4. Examine your action strategy and specify concrete steps on a timeline.

5. Share your vision statement and chosen activity plan with other groups.

6. Design and implement a ritual to celebrate your project of cultural rebirth.

7. Select a time for a follow-up meeting to report and celebrate your progress.

Earth Covenant
A Citizens' Treaty for Common Ecological Security

Preamble

We, the peoples of Earth, rejoice in the beauty and wonder of the lands, skies, waters, and life in all its diversity. Earth is our home. We share it with all other living beings. Yet we are rendering Earth uninhabitable for the human community and for many species of life. Lands are becoming barren, skies fouled, waters poisoned. The cry of people whose land, livelihood, and health are being destroyed is calling us to awaken. We and all living beings depend upon Earth and upon one another for our common existence, well-being, and development. Our common future depends upon a re-examination of our most basic assumptions about humankind's relationship to Earth. We must develop common principles and systems to shape this future in harmony with Earth. Governments alone cannot secure the environment. As citizens of the world, we accept responsibility in our personal, occupational, and community lives, to protect the integrity of Earth.

Principles and Commitments

In covenant with each other and on behalf of the whole Earth community, we commit ourselves to the following principles and actions:

Relationship with Earth: All life is sacred. Each human being is a unique and integral part of Earth's community of life and has a special responsibility to care for life in all its diverse forms. Therefore, we will act and live in a way that preserves the natural life processes of Earth and respects all species and their habitats. We will work to prevent ecological degradation.

Relationship with Each Other: Each human being has the right to a healthful environment and to access to the fruits of Earth. Each also has a continual duty to work for the realization of these rights for present and future generations. Therefore—concerned that every person have food, shelter, pure air, potable water, education, employment, and all that is necessary to enjoy the full measure of human rights—we will work for more equitable access to Earth's resources.

Relationship Between Economic and Ecological Security: Since human life is rooted in the natural processes of Earth, economic development, to be sustainable, must preserve the life-support systems of Earth. Therefore, we will use environmentally protective technologies and promote their availability to people in all parts of Earth. When doubtful about the consequences of economic goals and technologies on the environment, we will allow an extra margin of protection for nature.

Governance and Ecological Security: The protection and enhancement of life on Earth demand adequate legislative, administrative, and judicial systems at appropriate local, national, regional, and international levels. In order to be effective, these systems must be empowering, participatory, and based on openness of information. Therefore, we will work for enactment of laws that protect the environment and promote their observance through educational, political, and legal action. We shall advance policies of prevention rather than only reacting to ecological harm.

Declaring our partnership with one another and with our Earth, we give our word of honor to be faithful to the above commitments.[3]

For Meditation . . .
Teach us
To continue the Creation
To help the seeds
To multiply,
Giving good
For the people
And for the beasts.

Teach us
To further the joy
You never tire of offering
When weary travellers find you,
A signpost to their home.

Teach us
To make the horizon
Become a beautiful image
Of Creation's grandeur.

Teach us
To accept
The mediation of those
Who wish to unite us
To our fellows,
As you accept the gift
Of the water that binds
Land to land,
No matter how great
The distances!

What do you suffer
In the dust of deserts?
How do you look upon
Those of us who,
Though capable of transforming
The waste of lushness,
Prefer to be creators
Of barrenness?

And how do you rejoice
In the rain
That brings forth your fruits?
And what pain do you feel
At the storms
That drown you with floods,
Destroying plantations,
Crushing houses and the lives
Of animals, of plants, of people?

How great is the lesson
You give us,
O Earth,

More than sister:
Our mother Earth!

All our lives
We walk carelessly across you,
And when life leaves us,
With no shadow of resentment,
You open up to us
Your maternal bosom
To keep
Our flesh,
Our ashes,
For the joy
Of the resurrection.[4]

The leader's fundamental act is to induce people to be aware or conscious of what they feel—to feel their true needs so strongly, to define their values so meaningfully, so that they can be moved to purposeful action.[5]

Canticle for Earth

Earth Story, Sacred Story is:
Our interaction with the universe
   celebration and caring
   both personal and collective;
Ecological, holistic, and just;
A moral strategy of voluntary simplicity;
Passion and compassion for Earth;
   vision-packed, action-packed, and immediate;
An accountable media and new information systems
   to collapse consumerism;
Loving our planet during these fragile years;
Humans living on Earth in mutually enhancing ways;
Seeing the self as an aspect of a larger sacred community;
Awakening to the beauty and sound
   of the dawn, sunset, mountains, trees, and birds.

Earth Story, Sacred Story celebrates:
The authentic wisdom of all world religions;
The movement toward a deep change of heart;
A reverence for all creation
   that is born of awe, wisdom, and radical amazement;
Acknowledgment of and reflection on the patterns that connect;
A shared reverence for our common existence;
Newness in the context of joy;
Our collective potential to heal, birth, and transform;
Images that transcend cultures:
   A common language and common symbols
   in our common struggle;
Our remembrance of what is beautiful and new.

The forces that promote planetary survival;
Seeing our ecological self
   as profoundly connected to the whole of life;
The illusion that we are separate and fragile;
Seeing ourselves in relationship to the cosmos;
Patterns for healing people and the planet;
Healing any perceived conflict
   between the needs of the biosphere and "the street";
The intrinsic value of all life;
Diversity and interconnectedness
   in the natural world;
A passion for gender justice;
Prophetically tearing up and planting;
Moving out from communities of hope;
Remembering our history and origins;
Participating in an eco-psychology
   that heals our connection to people and the planet;
Embracing in peace our beauty and our wounds.

Earth Story, Sacred Story sees:
Our story as the story of Earth;
Cultural collapse and ecological devastation as a wasteland
   that will be
   the inheritance
   of our children;
Our challenge and response
   to the magnitude of the moment
   as rediscovering our destiny and call;
God in the cosmological order;
In the book of Earth a new language for a new era;
The wonderful fact that we are coded
   to be in relationship with all;
Dance, song, play, painting,
   writing, and movement
   as acts of solidarity with the natural world;
A spontaneous people for a new era
   as called to create a dream for the future;

A dream of beauty and action
  that liberates structures and evokes freedom;
A dream that will be born
  of experience and reflection;
A dream to celebrate competence and trust;
Reverence for diversity and uniqueness;
Re-energized mysticism and geo-justice;
A cosmic consciousness
  with full participation on every level;
Quality rather than control;
Spontaneity rather than power over;
Creativity rather than reproduction;
Innovation rather than imitation;
Union rather than separateness;
Prophecy rather than profits;
Interdependence honored
  with dualism critiqued.

Earth Story, Sacred Story invites us to:
Live in a world of harmony,
  balance, and peace;
Savor ecology and reverence
  and interconnectedness;
Melt alienation and respond with relatedness;
Find in each ending a new beginning,
  completion, and newness;
Foster the emergence of a New World Order
  that is healthy, generative, and whole;
Evoke a vision that is generous and just;
Follow our deepest fascinations;
Honor our intuitions;
Listen beyond words;
Balance vision and praxis;
Build webs, gatherings, and mediations of support;
Invent and envision a new culture
  as we celebrate Earth Story, Sacred Story.

Notes

Opening Quotation
1. Blanche Gallagher, *Meditations with Teilhard de Chardin* (Santa Fe, N.M.: Bear & Company, 1988), p. 133.

Introduction
1. *Hymn of the Universe* (New York: Harper Torchbooks, 1961), pp. 68-69.
2. Derry 2020 Vision Community Festival, 1989.

Chapter 1: The Unfolding Story
1. *Hero with a Thousand Faces* quoted in Sam Keen and Ann Valley-Fox, *Your Mythic Journey* (Los Angeles: Jeremy Tarcher, Inc., 1973), p. xiv.
2. Dag Hammarskjöld, *Markings* (New York: Alfred A. Knopf, 1970), p. 89.
3. In *God's Trombones: Seven Negro Sermons in Verse* (New York: Viking Press, 1927), p. 17.
4. Thomas Berry, *The Dream of the Earth* (San Francisco: Sierra Club Books, 1988), p. 132.
5. Michael Dowd, *EarthSpirit* (Mystic, Conn.: Twenty-Third Publications, 1991), p. 23.
6. Thomas Berry, *The Dream of the Earth*.
7. Erich Jantsch, *The Self-Organizing Universe* (New York: Pergamon Press, 1980).
8. This ritual was developed by Miriam Therese MacGillis of Genesis Farm in Blairstown, N.J.

Chapter 2: Creativity and Uniqueness
1. In John Roger and Peter McWilliams, *Do It* (Los Angeles: Prelude Press, 1991), p. 330.
2. In Blanche Gallagher, *Meditations with Teilhard de Chardin* (Santa Fe, N.M.: Bear & Co., 1988).
3. *The Prophet* (New York: Alfred A. Knopf, 1923), p. 21.
4. *Beyond Psychology* (New York: Dover Publications, 1958).
5. Rainer Maria Rilke, *Letters to a Young Poet* (San Rafael, Cal.: Classic Wisdom/New World Library, 1992).

Chapter 3: Interiority and Depth
1. *States of Grace: Spiritual Grounding in the Post-Modern Age* (Harper-SanFrancisco, 1991), p. 29.
2. Interview with Laurens van der Post, BBC.
3. *States of Grace*, p. 136.
4. *The Turning Point* (New York: Bantam New Age Books, 1982), p. 26.
5. Thomas Berry, C.P., in dialogue with Thomas Clarke, S.J., *Befriending the Earth: A Theology of Reconciliation Between Humans and the Earth*, Anne Lonergan and Stephen Dunn, eds. (Mystic, Conn.: Twenty-Third

Publications, 1991), p. 25.

6. Pierre Teilhard de Chardin, *The Divine Milieu* (New York: Harper &
Row, 1960), p. 75.

Chapter 4: Communion and Compassion

1. *The Universe Story* (HarperSanFrancisco, 1992), p. 77.
2. Paulo Friere, *Pedagogy of the Oppressed* (New York: Seabury Press, 1973),
pp. 36-41.
3. Quoted in Matthew Fox, *Original Blessing* (Santa Fe, N.M.: Bear &
Company, 1983), p. 286.
4. Quoted on card distributed at Martin Luther King, Jr. Center for Non-
Violence, Atlanta, Georgia.
5. Quoted in Wayne Simsic, *Earthsongs: Praying with Nature* (Winona:
Minn.: Saint Mary's Press, 1992), p. 5.
6. Rachel Carson, *The Edge of the Sea* (New York: Houghton Mifflin Co.,
1955).

Chapter 5: The Rebirth of Culture

1. *A New Vision of Reality* (Springfield, Ill.: Templegate Publishers, 1989), p. 1.
2. Quoted in Matthew Fox, *Meditations with Meister Eckhart* (Santa Fe, N.M.:
Bear & Company, 1981), p. 14.
3. Quoted in David Morris, *The Culture of Pain* (Berkeley, Cal.: University of
California Press, 1991), p. vi.
4. "Finding Heaven on Earth," interview with Thomas Berry by Michael
Hamer and Nathaniel Mead, *New Age Journal*, March/April, 1990, p.
135.
5. Rosemary Ruether, *New Woman, New Earth* (Seabury Press, 1975), p. 211.
6. Matthew Fox, *Creation Spirituality* (HarperSanFrancisco, 1991), p. 12.

Chapter 6: News from Planet Earth

1. *Earth Day—The Beginning*, compiled and edited by National Staff of
Environmental Action (New York: Arno Press, Bantam Books, 1970), p.
xvi.
2. Quoted by Bishop Thomas Gumbleton in address at University of
California at Berkeley, 1991.
3. Postcard published by Donnelly/Colt, Box 188, Hampton, CT 06427.
4. Quotes by Governor Mario Cuomo and Senator Bill Bradley, from
speeches at the 1992 Democratic Convention in New York City.
5. *The People Parish: A Model of Church Where People Flourish* (Notre Dame,
Ind.: Ave Maria Press, 1986).
6. *Markings* (New York: Alfred A. Knopf, 1970).
7. Friedrich Nietzche.
8. Thomas Merton in Jim Forest, *Living with Wisdom: A Life of Thomas
Merton* (Maryknoll, N.Y.: Orbis Books, 1991).

Chapter 7: A Spirituality of Earth

1. *The Path to Hope* (Maryknoll, N.Y.: Orbis Books, 1993), p. 107.
2. Ann Louise Gilligan, "Returning for the First Time," in *Faith and the
Intifada*, ed. Naim S. Ateek, Marc H. Ellis, and Rosemary Radford
Ruether (Maryknoll, N.Y.: Orbis Books, 1992), p. 189.
3. Dwight N. Hopkins and George Cummings, *Cut Loose Your Stammering*

Tongue (Maryknoll, N.Y.: Orbis Books, 1991), p. 100.
4. Esalen is an eclectic center for human growth and potential, founded in the early 1960s at Big Sur on California's Pacific Coast.
5. Quoted in *The Open Heavens* by Eugene Drewermann (Maryknoll, N.Y.: Orbis Books, 1991).

Chapter 8: Geo-Justice: A Preferential Option for Earth
1. Gary Snyder in *Earth Prayers from Around the World*, Elizabeth Roberts and Elias Amidon, eds. (HarperSanFrancisco, 1991), p. 43.
2. United Nations Environmental Sabbath Program.

Chapter 9: The Journey Into Gender
1. *Gaia and God* (HarperSanFrancisco, 1992), p. 1.
2. *The Complete Poems* (New York: Peter Kavanagh Hand Press, 1972), p. 81.
3. Editorial in the *South Bend Tribune*, South Bend, Indiana, March 29, 1993.
4. Chief Seattle, quoted in *Earth Prayers*, Elizabeth Roberts and Alias Amidon, eds. (HarperSanFrancisco, 1991), p. 10.

Chapter 10: Acting Globally and Locally
1. *A Theology of Liberation*, rev. (Maryknoll, N.Y.: Orbis Books, 1988).
2. Blanche Gallagher, *Meditations with Teilhard de Chardin* (Santa Fe, N.M.: Bear & Co., 1981), p. 119.
3. *Ibid.*, p. 133.
4. Joseph Donders, *Charged with the Spirit* (Maryknoll, N.Y.: Orbis Books, 1993).
5. Adrienne Rich, *The Dream of a Common Language, Poems 1974-77* (New York: W.W. Norton, 1978), p. 67.

Commencement
1. *On the Pulse of Morning* (New York: Random House, 1993).
2. These questions are from David Feinstein and Stanley Krippner, *Personal Mythology* (Los Angeles: Jeremy Tarcher, 1988), p. 14.
3. Global Education Associates, 475 Riverside Dr., Suite 1848, New York, N.Y. 10115.
4. Dom Helder Camara, *Sister Earth: Ecology & the Spirit* (New York: New City Press, 1990), p. 87.
5. James MacGregor Burns, quoted in *Cold Anger* by Mary Beth Rodgers (University of North Texas Press, 1990), p. 11.

Additional Resources

Alinsky, Saul. *Rules for Radicals*. New York: Random House, 1971.

Anderson, William. *The Green Man: The Archetype of Our Oneness with the Earth*. HarperSan Francisco, 1990.

Arnold, Patrick. *Wildmen, Warriors and Kings: Masculine Spirituality and the Bible*. New York: Crossroad, 1991.

Balasuriya, Tissa. *Planetary Theology*. Maryknoll, N.Y.: Orbis Books, 1984.

Bellah, Robert, et al. *The Good Society*. New York: Alfred A. Knopf, 1991.

Berry, Thomas. *The Dream of the Earth*. San Francisco: Sierra Club Books, 1988.

_____ (in Dialogue with Thomas Clarke, S.J.)., Anne Lonergan and Stephen Dunn, eds. *Befriending the Earth: A Theology of Reconciliation Between Humans and the Earth*. Mystic, Conn.: Twenty-Third Publications, 1991.

Boff, Leonardo, *Ecclesiogenesis: The Base Communities Reinvent the Church*. Maryknoll, N.Y.: Orbis Books, 1986.

Brown, Robert McAfee. *Gustavo Gutierrez: An Introduction to Liberation Theology*. Maryknoll, N.Y.: Orbis Books, 1990.

_____. *Liberation Theology*. Louisville: Westminster/John Knox Press, 1993.

Burch, Charles, William Eakin, Jay McDaniel, eds. *Liberating Life: Contemporary Approaches to Ecological Theology*. Maryknoll, N.Y.: Orbis Books, 1990.

Capra, Fritjof, and David Standl-Rast. *Belonging to the Universe*. HarperSanFrancisco, 1991.

Conlon, James. *Geo-Justice: A Preferential Option for the Earth*. Winfield, B. C.: Wood Lake Books; San Jose, Cal.: Resource Publications, 1990.

Culbertson, Philip. *New Adam: The Future of Male Spirituality*. Minneapolis: Fortress Press, 1992.

Cummings, Charles. *Eco-Spirituality: Toward a Reverent Life*. Mahwah, N.J.: Paulist Press, 1991.

Daly, Herman, and John Caleb, Jr. *For the Common Good: Redirecting the Economy Toward Community, the Environment and a Sustainable*

Future. Boston: Beacon Press, 1989.

Dorr, Donal. *The Social Justice Agenda: Justice, Ecology, Power and the Church.* Maryknoll, N.Y.: Orbis Books, 1991.

Dowd, Michael. *EarthSpirit: A Handbook for Nurturing an Ecological Christianity.* Mystic, Conn.: Twenty-Third Publications, 1991.

Driver, Tom. *The Magic of Ritual: Our Need for Liberating Rites That Transform Our Lives and Our Communities.* HarperSanFrancisco, 1992.

Edwards, Denis. *Made From Stardust.* Blackburn, Australia: Collins Dove, 1992.

Evans, Donald. *Spirituality and Human Nature.* Albany: State University of New York Press, 1993.

Ferguson, Duncan. *New Age Spirituality.* Louisville: Westminster/ John Knox Press, 1993.

Fowler, James. *Weaving the New Creation: Stages of Faith and the Public Church.* HarperSanFrancisco, 1991.

Fox, Matthew. *The Coming of the Cosmic Christ.* HarperSanFrancisco, 1988.

_____. *Original Blessing.* Santa Fe, N.M.: Bear & Co., 1981.

Fox, Warwick. *Toward a Transpersonal Ecology: Developing New Foundations for Environmentalism.* Boston and London: Shambhala Publications, 1990.

Franck, Frederick. *To Be Human Against All Odds.* Berkeley: Asian Humanities Press, 1991.

Freire, Paulo. *Cultural Action for Freedom.* Cambridge, Mass.: Harvard Educational Review, 1988.

_____. *Pedagogy of the City.* New York: Continuum, 1993.

_____. *Pedagogy of the Oppressed.* New York: Seabury Press, 1973.

Fritz, Robert. *The Path of Least Resistance.* New York: Ballantine, 1984.

Giroux, Henry. *Border Crossings: Cultural Workers and the Politics of Education.* New York: Routledge, 1992.

Gore, Albert. *Earth in Balance: Ecology and the Human Spirit.* Boston: Houghton Mifflin Co., 1992.

Griffiths, Bede. *A Return to the Center.* Springfield, Ill.: Templegate Publishers, 1976.

Grof, Stanislav. *The Holotropic Mind.* HarperSan Francisco, 1992.

Gutierrez, Gustavo. *We Drink From Our Own Wells.* Maryknoll,

N.Y.: Orbis Books, 1984.

Hart, John. *The Spirit of the Earth: A Theology of the Land.* Mahwah, N.J.: Paulist Press, 1984.

Hays, Edward. *Prayers for a Planetary Pilgrim: A Personal Prayer Manual for Prayer and Ritual.* Easton, Kans.: Forest Peace Books, 1989.

Heyneman, Martha. *The Breathing Cathedral: Feeling Our Way into a Living Cosmos.* San Francisco: Sierra Club Books, 1993.

Horton, Myles, and Paulo Freire. *We Make the Road by Walking.* Philadelphia: Temple University Press, 1990.

Horwitt, Sanford. *Let Them Call Me Rebel: Saul Alinsky, His Life and Legacy.* New York: Alfred A. Knopf, 1989.

Ingram, Catherine. *In the Footsteps of Gandhi: Conversations with Spiritual Social Activists.* Berkeley: Parallax Press, 1990.

Institute for Contextual Theology. *Third World Theology.* Johannesburg: Catholic Institute for International Relations, 1985.

Kaufman, Michael. *Cracking the Armor: Power, Pain and the Lives of Men.* Toronto: Viking/Penguin Books Canada, 1993.

Keen, Sam. *Fire in the Belly: On Being a Man.* New York: Bantam Books, 1991.

Kelleher, Patricia, and Mary Whelan. *Dublin Communities in Action: A Study of Six Projects.* Dublin: Community Action Network, 1992.

Kelly, Tony. *An Expanding Theology: Faith in a World of Connections.* Newton, N.S.W. Australia: E.J. Dwyer, 1993.

King, Thomas M. *Teilhard de Chardin.* Wilmington: Michael Glazier, 1988.

King, Ursula. *Toward a New Mysticism.* New York: Seabury, 1981.

LaChance, Albert. *Greenspirit: Twelve Steps in Ecological Spirituality.* Rockport, Mass.: Element, 1991.

Lappe, Frances Moore. *Rediscovering America's Values.* New York: Ballantine Books, 1989.

Lee, Bernard, and Michael Cowan. *Dangerous Memories: House Church and Our American Story.* Kansas City: Sheed and Ward, 1986.

Maser, Chris. *Global Imperative: Harmonizing Culture and Nature.* Walpole, N.H.: Stillpoint Publishing, 1992.

May, Rollo. *My Quest for Beauty.* Dallas: Saybrook Publishing, 1985.

McBrien, Richard. *Report on the Church: Catholicism After Vatican II.* San Francisco/New York: HarperCollins, 1992.

McCarthy, Scott. *Creation Liturgy: An Earth Centered Theology of Worship.* San Jose, Cal.: Resource Publications, 1987.

McDaniel Jay. *Earth, Sky, Gods & Mortals: Developing an Ecological Spirituality.* Mystic, Conn.: Twenty-Third Publications, 1989.

McDonagh, Sean. *To Care for the Earth: A Call to a New Theology.* Santa Fe, N.M.: Bear & Co., 1986.

_____. *The Greening of the Church.* Maryknoll, N.Y.: Orbis Books, 1990.

McFague, Sallie. *The Body of God: An Ecological Theology.* Minneapolis: Fortress Press, 1993.

Melville, Arthur. *With Eyes to See: A Journey from Religion to Spirituality.* Walpole, N.H.: Stillpoint Publishing, 1992.

Merton, Thomas. *Conjectures of a Guilty Bystander.* New York: Doubleday, 1966.

Miller, Ronald S., and Editors of *New Age Journal. As Above So Below: Paths to Spiritual Renewal in Daily Life.* Los Angeles: Jeremy P. Tarcher, 1992.

Moore, Thomas. *Care of the Soul: A Guide for Cultivating Depth and Sacredness in Everyday Life.* New York: HarperCollins, 1992.

Ormond, Neil. *Introducing Contemporary Theologies: The What and the Who of Theology Today.* Newton, N.S.W. Australia: E. J. Dwyer, 1992.

Phipps, John, and Frances Phipps. *The Politics of Inner Experience: Dynamics of a Green Spirituality.* London: Green Print, 1990.

Rahner, Karl. *The Practice of Faith: A Handbook of Contemporary Spirituality.* New York: Crossroad, 1992.

Rifkin, Jeremy. *Biosphere Politics.* New York: Crown Publishing, 1991.

Rockefeller, Steven, and John Elder, eds. *Spirit and Nature.* Boston: Beacon Press, 1992.

Rohr, Richard, and Joseph Martos. *The Wild Man's Journey: Reflections on Male Spirituality.* Cincinnati: St. Anthony Messenger Press, 1991.

Roof, Wade Clark. *A Generation of Seekers: The Spiritual Journey of the Baby Boom Generation.* HarperSanFrancisco, 1993.

Santouris, Elisabeth. *GAIA: The Human Journey From Chaos to Cosmos.* New York: Pocket Books, Simon & Schuster, 1989.

Schaef, Anne Wilson. *Beyond Therapy, Beyond Science: A New Model for Healing the Whole Person.* HarperSanFrancisco, 1992.

Scharper, Stephen, and Hilary Cunningham, eds. *The Green Bible.* Maryknoll, N.Y.: Orbis Books, 1993.

Sheldrake, Rupert. *The Rebirth of Nature: The Greening of Science and God.* New York: Bantam Books, 1991.

Shor, Ira, ed. *Freire for the Classroom: A Source Book for Liberatory Teaching.* Portsmouth, N.H.: Boynton/Cook-Heinemann, 1987.

Simsic, Wayne. *Natural Prayer: Encountering God in Nature.* Mystic, Conn.: Twenty-Third Publications, 1991.

Sjöberg, Leif, and W. H. Auden. *Dag Hammarskjold: Markings.* New York: Alfred A. Knopf, 1964.

Smillie, Ben. *Beyond the Social Gospel: Church Protest on the Prairies.* Saskatoon: Fifth House Publishers; Toronto: United Church Publishing House, 1991.

Sobrino, Jon. *Spirituality of Liberation: Toward Political Holiness.* Maryknoll, N.Y.: Orbis Books, 1990.

Tilby, Angela. *Soul: An Introduction to the New Cosmology: Time, Consciousness, and God.* London: BBC Education, 1992.

Trefil, James. *Reading the Mind of God: In Search of the Principle of Universality.* Garden City, N.Y.: Anchor Books/Doubleday, 1989.

Glossary

Communion - the compassionate bonding that extends through the entire earth community through gravitational interaction.

Community Organization and Development - a "bottom-up," fully democratic process of participation, relationship, listening, equality, dignity, curiosity, trust, and action that envisions our community as the sacred community of the natural world and our work as the great work of creation.

Compassion - the extension of a comprehensive bonding with Earth and its people through which we discover our original unity and interconnectedness.

Cosmology - the study of the universe as a whole, including its origins, evolution, and unfolding.

Creativity - the sacred impulse toward generativity that gives expression to diversity in the universe; a manifestation of uniqueness and surprise through multiple modes of human expression.

Creator - the conscious source of transformation; expresses self as principle of differentiation.

Cultural Rebirth - the process and story that reveal the three principles of the universe (differentiation, interiority, and communion) reflected in the dynamics of the Trinity; these tendencies when inculcated into the culture through creativity, depths, and compassion become a sacrament for the era that awaits us.

Culture - those "habits of the heart" that give expression to the entire Earth community through art, custom, values, beliefs, social structures, and story; patterns of trust by which individuals and groups interpret, evaluate, and reflect on their relationship to Earth and its people.

Depth - our capacity for profound experience, expression, and relationship within the Earth community through which our inmost self is intimately connected with the divine at the heart of all creation.

Differentiation - the uniqueness in the universe through which every creature is a particular manifestation of the divine with a specific gift and responsibility.

Earth - this dazzling array of beauty and life.

Earth Literacy - to read and write (reflect on and act authentically) in relationship to the entire Earth community; the capacity to foster and sustain more mutually enhancing relationships with Earth, through restoring ecological balance and restructuring political and economic relationships on the global level.

Ecology - the intricate web that life is, that greens all things as they interact with each other and Earth.

Evolution - natural change over a period of time that affirms that adaptation during life can be passed on to offspring and others.

Geo-Justice - a personal and planetary challenge to discover the converging terrain between ecological and social justice; a passionate and practical challenge through action to participate in the harmony, balance, and peace that Earth already knows.

Interiority - the capacity for deep experience that releases spontaneous energy to configure patterns of relationship and enhance inner articulation.

Mysticism - an awakening to an experience of oneness with the divine in which the experience, that which is experienced, and the process of the experience are one.

Popular Education - an approach that sees the awareness of reality and self awareness as one event; through critical reflection the consciousness of oppression dies to be reborn in freedom through authentic action to restore the environment and restructure society; a context in which Earth becomes the classroom.

Power - the ability to act fully from within and among the entire Earth community and to extend and awake this capacity in others from the ultimate source of strength that lies hidden in Earth.

Ritual - a process of empowerment and experimentation that engages us in a non-linear language of symbol and myth; an approach beyond words that unites our vision and action through silence, movement, music, and story.

Spirituality - a process of insight, experience, and expression through which we celebrate, change, remember, and act into the future; an awakening to the depths, the unfolding of our story with Earth in mind.

Story - purpose and coherence; we remember the sacred, our roots, and destiny as we reflect on the sequence of transformative moments that constitute the cosmos and ourselves.

Transformer (spirit) - the uncreated energy of unity that holds things in relationship.

Universe - all that is, including all space and matter.

Word - the source from which everything flows; the vehicle for expressing the inner articulation and interiority of things.

World Order - to develop and implement local and global approaches to planetary peace through research, reflection, and action in response to the mysterious forces and energies that guide life in an unplanned plan toward functional relationships within the entire Earth community.

Sacred Earth

With gratitude and grace
We celebrate the story
Of creation, liberation, and us.

In blessing and brokenness
We restore hunger for newness
Boiling from the wellsprings of our souls.

With courage and caring
We lament the consequence of loss
Yet rejoice to find again Sacred Earth.

Here within wonder and surprise
We rediscover hope
And recognize once more the signature of God.